Get
WEALTHY
$elling
Anything and
Everything

Alonza Cassie Brown

Creating Wealth through Salesmanship

Selling is One of the Highest Paid Professions in the World

Published by:
eBlessings.us
P. O. Box 601
Stone Mountain, GA 30086
www.info@eblessings.us
www.acbrown@eblessings.us

"Get Wealthy Selling Anything and Everything"
Including Daily Affirmations

Copyright © 2010 Alonza C. Brown and James Anthony Allen

All Rights Reserved. Printed in the United States of America.
Copyright © 2009 by Alonza C. Brown and eBlessings.
P.A.U.S.E.® is a registered trademark of Alonza C. Brown and James Anthony Allen. No part of this book may be reproduced, stored in a retrieval system, or transmitted by any means, electronic, mechanical, photocopying, recording, or otherwise, without written permission from the author.

For further information, you may write to above address or:

Alonza C. Brown
5533 Silver Ridge Drive
Stone Mountain, Georgia 30086

Scripture quotations from the Holy Bible, King James Version unless otherwise specified.

ISBN-10: 1456321196
ISBN-13: 9781456321192

Printed by BookSurge Publishing
North Charleston, South Carolina

Layout, design, editing, and cover design by:
J. Anthony Allen, eBlessings.us, Stone Mountain. Georgia

Alonza Cassie Brown's books and books from the eBlessings' Network are available at special quantity discounts for bulk purchases for sales promotions, premiums, fund-raising, or educational use. Special books, or book excerpts can also be created to fit specific needs. For details, write: Special Marketing, eBlessings, P.O. Box 601, Stone Mountain, GA 30086.

DEDICATION

This book is gratefully dedicated to

My wife:

Gladys R. Brown

My two sons:

Alonza C. Brown Jr.

Reginald M. Brown

and

all men, women, boys, and girls

who want to succeed in life

Table of Contents

ACKNOWLEDGEMENTS 9

INTRODUCTION 11

CHAPTER 1
You Sell All the Time 15
- How I Learned to Sell Anything (and Everything) 17
- Observe Your Mentor 22
- Week 1, Daily Sales Affirmations 26

CHAPTER 2
Sell Yourself 27
- Desire as the Mother of Motivation 29
- Fear as the Father of Motivation 31
- Yadkinville, NC 34
- Vocational Agriculture Contest 37
- Week 2, Daily Sales Affirmations 40

CHAPTER 3
Get the Know-How 41
- A Home Builder 43
- In Pursuit of Wealth 47
- Chapel Hill, North Carolina 50
- Week 3, Daily Sales Affirmations 53

CHAPTER 4
Overcome Your Obstacles 55
- Your Success in Selling 57
- Johnny Langston 59
- Home Builders Association 65
- Week 4, Daily Sales Affirmations 67

Table of Contents

CHAPTER 5
Walking Into a Setup **69**
- Arriving in Atlanta 71
- Getting Into Real Estate 74
- Hightower Road Apartments 79
- Week 5, Daily Sales Affirmations 87

CHAPTER 6
Words for the Wise **89**
- Use Intelligent Key Words And Statements 91
- Study, Rehearse, Approach, Close 97
- Week 6, Daily Sales Affirmations 101

CHAPTER 7
Sales Approach Insights **103**
- Professional Approaches 105
- Selling Anything and Everything 108
- Automobile Selling 115
- Week 7, Daily Sales Affirmations 120

CHAPTER 8
Insight on Closing the Sale **121**
- World's Greatest Sales Trainer 123
- Sow Service, Harvest Money 128
- Closing Apartment Home Leases 130
- Week 8, Daily Sales Affirmations 133

CHAPTER 9
Getting Your Referrals **135**
- Referrals 137
- The Six B's 141
- Pointers To Live By 143
- Week 9, Daily Sales Affirmations 145

CHAPTER 10
Professional Selling at Its Best 147
- Professional Selling..149
- Professional Sales Person..154
- An Informative Example..156
- Week 10, Daily Sales Affirmations............................161

CHAPTER 11
Trigger Your Customer's Imagination 163
- Taking Risks Using the Right Man............................165
- Apartments According to Income..............................169
- Earn As You Learn..172
- Rent to Buy...173
- Week 11, Daily Sales Affirmations............................175

CHAPTER 12
Wisdom In Business 177
- A Lot of Wisdom..179
- Choosing a CPA..181
- Dealing with Banks...182
- Choosing an Attorney..185
- A Comedy Show..187
- Week 12, Daily Sales Affirmations............................191

EPILOGUE 193
- Eleanor Thought She Had Security....................193

ACKNOWLEDGEMENTS

I worked nine hours a night putting myself through college. My father was a rich man; he wanted to send me to college. But I remembered right off what the Word says, "Acknowledge Him and He will direct your paths." The Lord spoke saying, "Work your way through college and let your father keep his money." This is exactly what I did and this is when my success started. You can start operating this way. Use your God-given gifts to create the life that you want.

I am 81 years of age and if I had another 48 years to travel this earth, I don't know what I would do differently. If I travel this earth another 48 years, I would have additional records of accomplishment to share with you. Use what I share with you in this book and you will have success beyond your imagination. If I can do it, so can you!

This book is going to teach you how to sell anything and everything including yourself. By reading and practicing the proven sales techniques found here, you can become successful financially in sales; whether you are selling now for a living or whether you have never thought about selling for a living.

Whatever your passion is, take a serious look at the opportunities within the pages of this book to fine-tune your business acumen. The information in this book will give you the tools to get the "Yeses" that are paramount.

Before the present economic downturn, people thought they could depend on that next paycheck. However, with so many pink slips and layoff notices handed out causing record-breaking unemployment, we have come to realize that there may not be a steady pay check. Do not panic. This book has your answer. Read this book and learn how

Acknowledgements

to overcome your fear of salesmanship. Learn to master selling products and services, instead of working that nine-to-five job at Joe's Meat Market or South East Corporate office. Practice this book's techniques and learn how not only to sell, but also to become a "profit center" for your business or for the company where you work.

The money is in sales. Name one business that you know that makes money without making a sale. Anyone can make money in sales when you learn the correct techniques, put them into practice and overcome the fear of meeting people. Learn to hire a "public relations representative" instead of putting an advertisement in the newspaper for a "sales associate."

Some people have the "gift of gab," great personalities or wonderful conversational skills. That does not have to be you. Do not worry about them. The minute you open your mouth, you are selling something. It might be yelling for the Atlanta Falcons, "Come on team!" but you are selling. You are selling that team. When you are standing at your office water cooler talking about how great your sports hero performed, you are selling that sports hero and that sport; and you are not making a dime out of it.

Pick a product or service, which is beneficial to someone or has that potential and talk about it—guess what—you are now selling. If you meet a rude person, remember, they have the problem, not you. Knock on doors, make some calls, have lunch, go to the country club, pull out those golf clubs and read this book. Read it not only once, but enough for the information to become a part of your daily conversation. Be motivated. Get out there and sell your product or service. Do not be afraid to knock on some doors.

Acknowledgements

The people who want your business are out there in the field. You or someone in your company must go out there and sell the people the benefits—the benefits of your products and services—or you have to get them into your store. In a nutshell, you have to go where the people are or get them to where you are. Next, you must get referrals and attempt to establish long-term relationships with your customer base. These relationships are the driving forces of any long-term successful business model.

You have made a great investment in yourself and your future with the purchase of this book. Now practice the professional sales techniques within these pages and see your success grow as you put in the effort and faith in your ability to offer individuals and businesses the opportunities that they are looking for in your products and services. It is great and amazing what people can do once given the opportunity.

INTRODUCTION

Many of you may know AC from his real estate days when "white flight" was beginning and at its paramount in Atlanta, Georgia. I am James Anthony Allen, Director of eBlessings (eBlessings.us), an international Internet interdenominational ministry and collaborator in this effort. Many people benefited from AC's "Jacob-like" sales techniques.

Before AC came to our home, the Holy Spirit said to me, "AC Brown is coming over." I thought and asked my wife, "Who is AC Brown? Do you know him? Is he that guy standing up praising God all the time at church?" Yes, that was him—AC Brown. During my life, the Holy Spirit may have told me only three times that someone was coming— this was one of those times. I knew something special was going to happen with this visit—P.A.U.S.E.® was revealed to me after four (4) years of working with AC; four tough long-suffering years.

When AC first came to the door he said, "The LORD told me to come here." I said, "The Lord told me that you were coming." He said, "The LORD said if you do not open the front door, I should go to the back door. If you and Allen have a falling out (and there were many—but the Holy Spirit directed me to keep working with him) go to the back door and keep knocking." AC also told me this. He said, "Allen, I have been a millionaire three times, each time the LORD told me to stick with a specific person and I would make millions." "Allen," he said, "this time the LORD told me to *'Stick with Allen,'* and I am going to do just that.

Introduction

Alonza C. Brown owned and rented single-family homes; additionally, he built and owned apartment home communities. He made fortunes and this book is to teach you the sales techniques, which took him to the top of his field.

AC is <u>imparting</u> his sales techniques to give families a way to "fish" before and after the pay check is no longer there. He is giving people an opportunity to learn how to make a livelihood selling something (because we all are always selling something.

AC is bringing to you what he has learned during his forty-eight (48) year track record of selling and teaching people to sell. He will tell you in a minute, "If you don't try anything, you will surely fail. You have to try something to see if it will work for you."

AC says, "Everyone is selling something all the time. When they open their mouths, they are selling something. Why not make selling a career? This is a great opportunity for you to solve all of your financial problems. AC is selling you this book, which is filled with ways for you to do just that—feed yourself and your family. Enjoy reading this book as Alonza C. Brown imparts his wisdom to you.

Get Wealthy $elling Anything and Everything

Alonza C. Brown

CHAPTER 1

You Sell All the Time

Chapter 1

You Sell All the Time

How I Learned to Sell Anything (and Everything)

For 48 years I've heard people make statements like this. "If I had the proper education..." Or "If I were not born with the color of this skin, I could succeed in life." "If I were only thinner... smarter... or prettier." In this book I will teach you how I was able to learn to sell anything. Early in my life I learned to listen and observe those around me to development an acumen of sales success. These sales techniques will help you with your sales objectives, goals and sales volumes. I have done it this way for over forty-eight (48) years. If I can do it this way, you can too.

My success started my senior year in high school. In high school I was labeled just a good old school bus driver. The principal of the high school was excited about having a speaking contest with members of the senior class before graduation. He brought the teachers from the Caucasian school to judge this contest. This I thought was unusual.

I never had the opportunity to practice with my classmates before the contest, because I drove a school bus during that class period. I practiced at night at home before a mirror; sometimes as late as twelve midnight or one am. On the day of the contest, the judge stood and said, "Ladies and gentlemen, we have heard some good speakers today, but we have unanimously agreed that our first place speaker is Alonza C. Brown."

Winning that speaking contest changed my life completely. It increased my self-confidence. It boosted my ego and gave me incentive to seek success through goal setting. It made me feel good about myself. Remember this always, in high school I was labeled "just a good old school bus driver." But before I left that stage that day as the good old school bus driver that I was, <u>I made up my</u>

mind that very day that everything I would touch in life from this point forward would turn to gold.

Remember what I said – I was in high school driving a school bus. I did this to make extra money. If I can do it this way, you can too. And it is not too late to make that decision to start—to start selling. Make a decision to make a change in your life through sales and through increasing your current sales and magnifying your sales potential. Why did I make this decision to go into sales instead of sticking to my nine-to-five job? How could I make this decision?

I realized that everyone and their brother were selling something the moment they opened their mouths. I decided I was going to use the same techniques I used to win that speaking contest—aggressiveness towards my goals and believing in myself when others did not. You can do it the way I did it and be on your way to being a highly successful sales person. Before you realize it you will be on your way to being a sales person who can earn hundreds of thousands of dollars. Receive the real success that you are looking for—you can find it in sales.

The question is: How did I win that speaking contest? My sister-in-law Ruth Brown, a real-life Saint, taught me at home at night by the mirror.

"Alonza," Ruth Brown my sister-in-law said to me in

one of her training sessions, "if you want to win that speaking contest, you need to observe your father Sam Brown."

Here is where I became acutely aware of practicing speeches. I would realize after my speech how positive the effects of a successful speech could be.

I would write out my presentation. I would read it over and over again until I became familiar with it. You have to learn it. No one knows that your sales speech is memorized. You cannot adlib the sales presentation, because it will not work. It has to be practiced until it becomes a part of you. Not that part of you that goes to church on Sunday, but that part of you that is with you all day long; seven days a week, twenty-four hours a day.

People are doing the same old things the same old ways. Writing it down, listening to the CD once, putting it down, going home, getting out of the car and continuing to do it the same old way. Aren't you tired of this program? If you are not getting the results you want, you must do it a different way. Do something with your life differently. Do not leave your husband. Do not leave your wife. But leave that non-successful place where you are and pick up selling. It will be the best financial decision you will have made in your life.

I became serious about practicing speeches with their specific effects in my mind, i.e., I practiced speaking with results in mind. I learned later in life that a sales presentation is only a speech and a good sales presentation could feed my family. I further understood that if I could eat off a *"good"* sales presentation, that if I had a *"great"* sales presentation, not only could I feed my family, but my extended family members as well.

What is going on all over this land is this. People are sitting in board meetings—bored to death. People are sitting in sales meetings—not learning much if anything. People are riding public transportation—not going anywhere fast. People are driving their clunkers—hopeful that the next raise will afford them better transportation. People are sitting in churches receiving new sermons, new messages—but going back home to the same old circumstances. Motivational speakers are bringing new ideas to their audiences which do not increase their wealth, only the wealth of the lecturer.

The problem is—most people are sitting there, listening, riding, driving, but still living life the same old way when they go home. They go home to that same old rut that is waiting for them. Selling gives everyone an opportunity to help another person by supplying their lives with the benefits of the product or service which they are selling.

Why live life the same old way, at the same old time? Enjoy the many benefits of selling. Selling is for everyone, many do not realize this—everyone sells something when they open their mouths. Do not allow poor habits, bad habits, old habits and other folks habits stop you from benefiting from the success which is yours if you only go out there and work for it. Think of it this way. Your fortune lies in the pockets of another person—go out there and work for what is yours.

Use this book to <u>learn to make a decision which will change your life</u> and the lives of your families by beginning to live life using the sales techniques and approaches found in this book. This will guarantee your success—and get you out of that personal rut, that economic rut, or that employment rut. <u>Apply these sales approaches, closes and sales techniques to improve your daily living with focused personal and business goals</u>.

ಸಿ ಲ

Observe Your Mentor

I want you to understand my gears changed that morning through Ruth Brown. When that gear shifts -- we begin to go in another direction. This is your opportunity to turn your sales from south to north. Turn your sales around with the sales experiences presented in these pages. I'm here to testify to you that when that gear shifts, the Creator is changing the direction in which He wants you to travel. Listen to what Ruth Brown said to me.

"Alonza, if you want to win that speaking contest, you need to observe your father Sam Brown."

That was all she said, but that was a mouthful.

If I was not in the mind of listening to my elders, I would have missed that gear shifting. I knew from the moment Ruth Brown told me to observe my father Sam Brown that those gears were shifting. I heard that gear shifting and I made a decision to step on life's accelerator.

We'll miss that gear shifting almost every time if we don't stay positive, stay prepared, and stay focused on the goal. These are winning habits that must be developed. Listen for that gear shift—be positive, get prepared and stay prepared, and keep focusing on the goals. It will be the best habit you'll ever develop in life. <u>Keeping our minds on our goals is the habit we want to develop</u>. Keeping your mind off of negative things—that is—focus on the positive and leave the negative wherever it was before it entered your mind. Now, you are heading in the right direction.

Why was I to observe Sam Brown? Sam Brown sent seven of my sisters and brothers to college. This was during the Depression Years. He had four girls in college at the same time, and he was only a farmer. I never heard this farmer say he didn't have any money. Sam Brown paid off his 98-acre farm in the 1920's, when many were losing their farms. He also paid for his children's college tuitions in the middle of the Depression years. Sam Brown was doing something right. He had my interest then, much like now, I should have your interest.

I would see him standing in the fields with five vocational agriculture teachers; both African-American and Caucasian brothers who came to seek his advice about farming from all over the entire state of North Carolina, or so I thought.

One day I asked him, "How can you spend all that time with county agents and vocational agricultural teachers?" I asked him how could he do it and take care of the farm and his family?

He gave me a curious look, although he had a smile on his face -- a serious smile. I will never forget it.

He said, "I can't afford not to help them."

I said, "You're not making a dime out of this."

And then he said to me, "<u>The way you get success in life is to be more concerned about others than you are about yourself</u>." Then Sam Brown said, "That is why I cannot afford not to help them."

Remember this about Sam Brown, he would walk his 98 acres of farmland tagging very special trees, shrubs, flowers, or fruit trees so he could later come back, dig them up and take them to the market or a local neighborhood for sale. <u>You must be resourceful, creative, energetic, and have a willingness to try new things</u>.

Week 1—My Daily Sales Affirmations

1. I will practice listening and observing those around me to development the business acumen of sales success.
2. I will set goals to make my success a reality.
3. I understand that everyone and their brother are selling something the moment they open their mouths.
4. I will be acutely aware of how I speak and practice speaking correctly.
5. I will practice making decisions, which will help make my life be more successful.
6. I will improve my daily living using focused personal and business goals applying the sales approaches, closes, and techniques in this book.
7. I will form a habit of keeping my mind on my goals as I move towards my success.
8. I will show my concern for others by offering them the benefits of what I am selling.
9. I will be more resourceful, creative, energetic, and have a willingness to try new things.

(Proven Techniques from AC Brown's 48-Year Track Record)

CHAPTER 2

Sell Yourself

Chapter 2

Sell Yourself

Desire as the Mother of Motivation

Many summers ago when I was younger, before marriage, I was visiting my wife's hometown of Wilson, North Carolina. I had been driving all day when we arrived. You know I was tired. Mrs. Ruffin, my wife's mother, 80 years of age at the time, came to me.

"Brown, take me to Wilson. I have 48 dozen eggs to take up there and some collard greens. I would like Gladys to come along with us."

Mrs. Ruffin was selling right then and I didn't know it. She knew that I would do just about anything to spend time with her daughter, so all she had to do was ask.

She knew <u>I was motivated by my desire</u> to please her and her daughter. She knew that all she had to do was ask and I would come "a running".

In sales, you always focus on benefits. She focused on my benefit when she asked Gladys to come along while giving me the opportunity to impress Gladys' mother. Now my wife knew I was a "catch" but I didn't know it at the time and I believed that I had to prove myself to her. In relationships as well as in life's situations and circumstances, <u>there is always a "silver lining"</u>.

In this book that "silver lining" is called a benefit. In your life experience, that silver lining may look like a negative circumstance, but it is only a silver lining in disguise. One only has to stay positive and look for the positive in each and every situation to see that silver lining.

The way Mrs. Ruffin said it, I was under the impression that these eggs were already sold and we were only making a delivery. I thought it was just a matter of taking Mrs. Ruffin to Wilson and unloading those eggs and collard greens; then turn around and head back. That is what I thought. Wrong. Mrs. Ruffin was selling.

When we arrived in Wilson, in this one-horse town, Gladys and I sat in the car talking. I noticed Mrs. Ruffin going door-to-door. I realized she was carrying dozens of eggs along with those collard greens trying to sell them one door, then the next; then another door and another.

Wait a minute! I thought. I had to do something, even though I was tired and sleepy.

Fear as the Father of Motivation

If desire is the mother of motivation, then fear is the father of motivation. Remember with Mrs. Ruffin I thought I was just being the driver. She had other ideas. When I saw Mrs. Ruffin waddling slowly up those steps to those houses—one by one, house by house—I knew that I would be there all day, or what was left of the day if I didn't do something immediately. Suddenly I thought, "fresh country eggs."

Know this; I was prepared for this situation without knowing it. <u>Preparation is key to what you are doing or what you are planning to do</u>. Sam Brown prepared me for this situation when I walked with him in downtown Roanoke Rapids on the weekends and in its neighborhoods selling fruit, vegetables, and anything he could get out of those 98 acres of land he owned.

Now, hear these words – *"fresh country eggs."* I knew

how to fill in the blanks. I reached in the automobile. I got a couple of baskets of eggs and I put them under my arm, along with some collard greens. I proceeded down the street yelling loudly.

"*Fresh country eggs, fresh country eggs. Come get your fresh country eggs.*"

If I can do it this way, you can too. I went as far as to spray water on those collard greens before I placed them under my arm, so they would look as fresh as possible.

CROWDS CREATE SALES

Children playing football in the street, stopped their game, ran into their homes to bring their mothers out to buy those eggs. Why did they stop playing football and go get their mothers? I asked them to do it. <u>Be motivated and do things which you up until now were afraid to do</u>. Open your mouth and try something differently.

Fear motivated me to get into action. I was afraid that if I waited on Mrs. Ruffin to deliver those eggs then I would have spent the rest of the day, which I was planning to spend with Gladys only, with Gladys and her mother "methodically-moving" selling eggs and collard greens.

Mothers came from all directions; some had money and some did not. Do not turn anyone away when you are selling. You want to create crowds, because crowds do create sales. You want to draw as many people to your product as possible; this increases your sales potential.

When the mothers came out of those houses, I simply asked them, "Two dozen or three?" The beauty of the whole thing is that they came out. Don't ever forget this – <u>excitement and crowds do create sales</u>. My voice was excited when I yelled *"fresh country eggs."* I was truly excited because I realized the faster I could move those eggs and greens, the faster I could spend some alone time with Gladys.

There was a man crossing the intersection on a bicycle. He heard me yelling, "fresh country eggs". He made a u-turn, came back, and bought a dozen eggs. There was also a man at the top of a 50-foot power pole. He stopped his repair work, climbed down and bought two dozen eggs.

That's not the end of the story. The end of this story goes like this. There was also a man directly across the street in front of where I was selling all these eggs. He too was selling eggs. He came over very quickly.

"How much are you getting for your eggs?" He asked.

And do you know what he discovered? He discovered

that I was getting more per dozen for my eggs than he. Furthermore, I was selling more eggs than he. And I still believe today, if I had just asked him to buy some of my eggs, he would have bought some of my eggs due to my enthusiasm and excitement. We had people coming up to us to purchase eggs like they were going to church. To say the least, Mrs. Ruffin was more than pleased with me. She talked about that experience for many years.

Yadkinville, NC

You have to persevere. You have to learn that you must continue to pursue your goals even though those around you and perhaps your circumstances are telling you that you must not go forward but stop and turn around—or more realistically, someone—namely your wife or your husband is telling you to stop selling and start working a nine-to-five job. A nine-to-five- job can be death to your financial security: D-E-A-T-H. But at that time I did not know this. I was looking for that nine-to-five to support my family financially.

I was hired as a vocational agriculture teacher in Yadkinville, North Carolina, a small town in Yadkin County, 80 miles west of Greensboro, North Carolina. I had a year round job with travel pay. They only hired me for one year because of my experience as a teacher. The Principal of the Yadkin County High School and the Superintendent of Schools had a good time laughing at my "C" and "D" transcript when I went to apply for the job. They sat there and laughed right in front of me. Can you believe that?

Understand me now, they only hired me for one year. They didn't believe in me. This was one of those times when I had to believe in myself. You will have those times also; when no one believes you can do it but you. Y-O-U: You are sometimes the only person that you can depend on to believe in you. Remember this: believe in you, believe in yourself from the top of your head to the bottom of your feet. Believe in what you are doing— believe in it completely. Believe it so you can achieve it. If you do not believe you can do a thing, why are you even trying? Do not just try a thing, do it.

> **Stop Sitting on the Sidelines**
>
> **Life will Take on a New Meaning**

The Principal of the Yadkin County High School and the Superintendent of Schools wanted to try me out to see if I could teach vocational agriculture at their school and in their county; after all I wasn't really a "country boy" or so they thought. I needed a job and I knew that I could do this one. I would work at the high school until 12:00 noon, then from 12:00 noon until about 5:00 p.m. I was on the farm working with the farmers.

Now I want you to understand that this was a new vocational agriculture department. This was to be the first year for their new teacher, AC Brown, and the first year his new farm boys would be attending this new high profile school facility. When I walked out of that Principal's office with the Superintendent of Schools standing there, I told God that I would be the best vocational agriculture instructor that ever walked into a school in North Carolina. If I can make a statement like this and believe it—you can too!

Stop sitting on the sidelines and get into the game. Stop sitting on the sidelines, depressed and waddling in self-pity. Stay away from people that are negative and do not have your best interest at heart. Be your own cheerleader. <u>Push through the disbelievers.</u> <u>You will never know if you can do a thing if you do not attempt it</u>. Do not allow others to keep you from starting a successful career in sales. Do it! Do it today!

Vocational Agriculture Contest

One **of the wonderful things** about this contest which was planned for the end of the school year is that it gave rural children an opportunity to compete on stage in several areas such as: speaking, grooming, teamwork, singing, academics, and poetry. Vocational agriculture teachers and their farm boys came to the Yadkin County High School from all over the entire state of North Carolina; twenty-five high schools participated.

That's right. The 25th one was Yadkin County High School. There were several areas in which the farm boys participated. One of the areas was quartet singing. I didn't know anything about teaching my students to sing. My job as a vocational agriculture teacher was to work at the high school teaching academics, then head to the farm to teach application to the farmers. It was difficult not to get involved in all the side issues associated with the job dealing with these farmers. In the meantime, I had a serious problem. I had to put that quartet together.

I had to be resourceful. Moreover, you have to be resourceful also. That is why this book is so beneficial. It gives you many resourceful tools to use to meet your hurdles head-on, to overcome those obstacles which show up, and teaches you how to set and meet realistic sales goals.

I told a local music teacher about my problem. She told me to bring the boys to her classroom in the afternoon on Fridays to practice.

"I won't charge you a thing," she said. "I will be glad to do it."

All you have to do is to be willing to take one step and the next direction will magically be in front of you. That next sales opportunity will come and all you have to do is be prepared and follow these "tried and true" sales approaches and closes.

It took very little effort on my part to make our program blossom. Not only did the music teacher get my farm boys to vocalize in tune, but she also told them what to wear. Those black shiny patent leather shoes, those black pants and white coats went well with my choreography. They broke out there singing, "Oh, Donna." The big afros were blowing in the wind, those four farm boys glided onto the stage, wailing away on *"Oh, Donna."* The crowd went wild.

Ladies and gentlemen you may be surprised at what you can get done when you apply yourself after proper preparation. I can tell you that I will not be surprised at what any of you can do after reading this book and applying its principles. Read this book more than once for these sales techniques to stick in your gut and become a part of you.

Guess who was there at the contest? The Principal of the Yadkin County High School and Superintendent of Schools. The same ones who had had such a good time laughing at my transcript. Remember they only hired me for one year. Guess what took place that day?

The Yadkin County High School farm boys, my Yadkin County farm boys, won the competition. In fact, they won all five areas. I had only one year of teaching vocational agriculture under my belt. Vocational agriculture teachers who had been teaching for years, some of them 20 and 30 years watched the Yadkin County High School farm boys walk away with the awards.

Believe in yourself when others do not believe in you. If you believe in yourself, others have a tendency to believe in you also. Grades are a means to an end, but are not the end in itself. Believe in yourself.

Week 2 – My Daily Sales Affirmations

1. I will find a product or service which I know will benefit others. My personal and sales goals motivate me.
2. In life, I understand I must take advantage of the opportunities, which come before me.
3. I know that preparation is a key to what I am doing or what I am planning to do.
4. I will study, research, and learn everything possible about this product or service. I will write my presentations and practice, practice, practice.
5. I will be motivated to do things, which until now I was afraid to do.
6. I understand that excitement and crowds do create sales, therefore I will incorporate excitement in my sales approach.
7. My knowledge and preparation will prepare me to be highly successful in my new endeavor.
8. I will push through the disbeliefs of others as I travel down the path to success.

(Proven Techniques from AC Brown's 48-Year Track Record)

CHAPTER 3

Get the Know-How

Chapter 3

Get the Know-How

A Home Builder

It is difficult, to say the least, to be successful without knowing something. You must know something to get somewhere. You must at least know where you are going so you can get there and so you can get there on time. You must set goals. The way to get and build wealth is to follow the proven sales and "personality" techniques found in this book as you apply them to your goals. You are going to learn by either reading, listening, or doing. I have done the work for you and now all you have to do is read, receive, and put what you have learned and what I am teaching you into action.

That gear was shifting on me again. This time it was my own doing which caused it to happen. But it was happening. I was now in the 9 to 5 job market, which many of you may be in—looking for or working in a J-O-B. Bruce Ruffin, my brother-in-law was building houses all over Greensboro, North Carolina.

I did not go to work for Bruce, but I knew I wanted to go into another industry other than teaching. In life, it is important to know that if you desire to go into a specific field of endeavor, you must learn as much as possible about that industry. I wanted to be a builder. Bruce was the perfect mentor. Bruce could tell you anything and everything about building a house. If anyone had any type of problem with building a house, Bruce had the answer. Bruce was the house construction "answer man."

I had the perfect mentor right there in our family. You may have your perfect mentor in your family as well. Do your due diligence, do your research. Find your mentor and grow rich in knowledge and know-how. <u>Do well by spending time with someone who has the know-how you would like to have.</u>

I got a job in Greensboro, North Carolina, working at P. Lori Lard cigarette factory from 11:00 pm to 7:00 am in the morning inhaling tobacco dust. I was a white collar man stepping into a blue collar job. Many of you are out there and you will not take that job because it is too dirty, too smelly, too many whites work there or too many blacks. This was a dirty, nasty job and I worked it.

Now here I am, working my plan to become a home builder by working in a cigarette factory at night—go figure. But that was all a part of the plan. People were not using words like "mentor" at that time, but in unspoken words, Bruce was now my mentor.

> **Do not Deviate from Your Plan**

While I inhaled tobacco dust, I imagined building houses; single family homes on vacant lots, then sub-divisions, apartments and more. Any idle time as well as busy time was filled with thoughts about my plans. <u>Imagination is key to your successes</u>. See it in your mind's eye. I could see concrete being poured, asphalt being poured for new streets, and new homes being built by AC Brown. <u>I imagined homes being built by AC Brown. I imagined subdivisions being developed by AC Brown.</u>

Mind you, I did not have the money and would never make enough money in this job to succeed in my dreams, in my goals. When I was with Bruce we talked building. When I would ride with him in his truck he talked building houses. All day long if possible, I would engage Bruce to learn anything and everything about building and selling houses. I rode with Bruce for days, and weeks, then months. We talked building houses all day long. I learned a lot. I believe Bruce did too.

At the time, there were many builders in the city. Bruce was not the most outstanding builder, but he was the man for the job. I arranged my schedule to stick with him. Remember, success is normally not something that happens overnight. You must work at it, plan for it, and imagine it. Just take it one step at a time.

※ ※

When I finally got up the courage to go into the big time building business, financing was a critical issue. Where was I going to get financing? You may be asking yourself that very same question: Where am I going to get the money I need to do what I desire to do?

As I said two years passed as I waited; tiring daily of inhaling tobacco dust and cleaning tar and nicotine off filthy tobacco machinery. You have to want it so badly that you allow nothing to change your path. Once you are on that path, there is no such thing as failure.

I sold my home in which I was living with my wife and son in order to get some startup money. One does what one must do to accomplish one's goals. Do whatever it takes to accomplish your goals. You may have something that you can sell to get your start up money. People wondered why we were selling a relatively new home. You cannot be concerned about what others are thinking and saying.

Your path represents your goals, the direction, which you are following—allow nothing to change that. Success will be yours if you stick to your program—stick to your goals. Doing it this way, I earned a million dollars three times. I had to <u>go out there and work for it</u>. Get up, get out, and do it. You may make some mistakes but keep going.

In Pursuit of Wealth

One day, just out of the blue, in walks RJ Hancock. RJ had been talking with Bruce about building and financing. Bruce had told him about me. He had told him that I needed money in order to move forward. RJ wanted to make sure that I was a man that he could trust, should he made me a loan.

Unknown to us at the time, RJ Hancock was also interested in building houses in a small town called Chapel

Hill, North Carolina. He was seeking us for information. He wanted our vision and our building know-how. We wanted his money to finance our homes. He asked many, many questions, then finally gave me a loan on just a handshake. The ease of financing really got me started—no collateral, no credit check, and no Dun and Bradstreet report.

If you have what people need, you operate from a "power position." <u>If you have the "know-how" the pursuit of your goals can be easier</u>. There are many people in your life who have what you need. There are also other people in your life who need what you have. <u>Study others in your preparation for life's goals.</u> You can learn so much from others if you would only ask. People love to talk. You will find that people will be more than happy to tell you all about how they made a fortune, accomplished a thing, or was successful in an endeavor. If nothing else, it builds their egos.

Upon giving us the first loan, he immediately set up an appointment to meet with Bruce Ruffin and me every Friday afternoon at 3:00 o'clock. He would ask us many questions. He was in the lumber business, but he never asked questions relating to lumber -- <u>never</u>! Not one question ever about the lumber business. Bruce and I were too close to the forest to see the trees, but RJ would soon show them to us as lumber.

RJ was asking a ton of questions about building—not about lumber mind you—but about building houses.

"Bruce," he would ask, "what do you think about *this* issue concerning the building business?"

"Brown," he would ask, "what about *that* issue concerning the building business?"

You have got to understand that in life there is no such thing as a free lunch. No one just walks into the office of another person in America and offers him an opportunity to borrow large sums of money without a cause or purpose. Our financial needs were so great that we could not see that RJ had a motive. We didn't know that he was in the learning business—he was learning as much as he could about the home building business while we boasted in our 1960's egos, thinking we were on top of the world. RJ was a blessing and just what we needed to continue to move forward. You see, we could only borrow a maximum of 13,000 from local banks.

> Use good insight and proper planning to secure your future.

Several months slipped by—nine months in fact. Every Friday, right on time, RJ showed up with a check and with an ear for listening. He listened as we shared our knowledge and expertise. We were enthusiastic about his visits even though we knew we were paying him "through the nose" in interest.

You can learn from anyone if you learn to see every one and every situation as a potential resource. You then can ask the right questions of your resource and listen for good responses. RJ saw us as resources. Learn to sell by listening and following the sales techniques in this book. They work. When selling anything, look to the industry leader and ascertain the positive characteristics of their business or their sales successes. Imitation is the highest form of flattery. Imitate someone who sells well. Find someone who sells well. Offer to help them without pay as you learn approaches, closes, and get better and better.

Chapel Hill North Carolina

We closed many loans with RJ Hancock. Life was good. Life was great! We knew that we had hit the big time. We were big time. That money from RJ was not only good for our business, but for our egos as well.

One Friday afternoon at 3:00 o'clock, RJ Hancock came in very excited. He invited us to go with him to Chapel Hill. He was dressed for the occasion. He could hardly wait to show us his new subdivision. We saw many houses under construction – signs swinging everywhere – "RJ Hancock Construction Company." He had put our ideas and experience to work for him.

This was a win-win situation. He was building homes like mad. We were so happy for him. I think that experience might have added 10 years to his life. RJ Hancock came into my life to get me started with my dream of building houses. I was happy that I was able to give back and make his dreams come true as well.

I went on to win the prestigious North Carolina Home Builders Association "Parade of Homes" Award for the Home of the Year, located today in Greensboro, North Carolina. You see, our association together made winners of all of us. If you keep a good attitude and help one another, everyone wins.

సు ఇ

Several months passed and the gear shifted again. My banker called me and said, "Mr. Brown, we can reduce the interest that you are paying and give you loans at a lower interest rate than you are now paying, if you can show me $10,000 in your checking account."

The gear shifted that morning. I made one more trip to RJ Hancock's office and borrowed the $10,000. I bade him farewell on that day.

I am saying something, which I know: <u>In your business, you have to do something</u>. If you do nothing, you will accomplish the same: N-O-T-H-I-N-G, nothing. Before you can accomplish anything, you have to have the guts and the nerve to move in. You have to "prime the pump" with something to get something. <u>You have to "prime the pump" with action for reaction to happen</u>. Keep your actions as well as your conversation positive and positive things will happen in your life, in your goals, and in your sales.

From that day to this day, I haven't had to use the services of RJ Hancock anymore. If I can do it this way, you can too!

Week 3 – My Daily Sales Affirmations

1. I understand that imagination is a key to my success. I will imagine the success, which I desire.
2. I will spend time with someone who has the expertise I would like to have. I will find a perfect mentor.
3. I will be patient and persevere as I follow my plans.
4. I will apply what I know and work hard and smart for my success.
5. I realize that if I have the expertise, the pursuit of my goals can be easier.
6. I will practice learning to see every one and every situation as a potential resource or opportunity.
7. I realize that I have to "prime my sales pump" with action before reaction will happen.
8. I will create a good relationship with each of my clients.
9. I will learn to forgive myself and forget my poor sales performances of the past. I will always work for self-improvement.
10. When I make a sale, I will always save a small percentage for future investments.

(Proven Techniques from AC Brown's 48-Year Track Record)

CHAPTER 4

Overcome Your Obstacles

Chapter 4

Overcome Your Obstacles

Your Success in Selling

Regardless of what you do for a living, whether you are employed or not, the proven sales techniques shared with you in this book, work. There is a path in every career field to follow which leads to business success—that path is sales. You can make the most perfect product that ever existed, but if no one knows about it and no one purchases it, then the product can not and will not pay for its very own existence. So you see, someone has to sell that product for it to have a viable product life. A successful product life means the product has to have a good sales track record, i.e., a good salesperson.

If you follow the sales paths in any industry, they will lead you to the personal sales successes you desire. Every industry needs a salesperson as noted by almost every industrial leader. The sales techniques outlined in this book show you how to follow these paths to success, which lead to increased sales, increased productivity and increased success. It works for every field into which you go regardless of your educational level or experience.

Any man, woman, boy or girl, who uses the sales techniques outlined in this book every day, seven days a week, will have success in any field of endeavor. No man on earth can compete with you unless he is doing it this way also. I don't care what you do for a living these proven techniques work. I don't know about you, but I want everything that's rightfully mine and you should, too. I am talking about your success here. Do you want your success or don't you? You must <u>have a desire for success</u>.

It is not the color of our skin that holds us back; nor is it our unattractiveness or weight. <u>What holds us back are the procedures which we know about or do not know about</u>. <u>What holds us back are the procedures that we use or do not use; or the choices we make or do not make</u>. I am giving you the procedures that worked for me for over forty-eight years. They worked very well for me and they will work very well for you also.

When we do not see our sales techniques working, do not get into a pity-party too quickly—not at all is my suggestion to you. Try to fine-tune your sales techniques before getting into a pity-party. Pity-parties block people's ideas. Positive mental attitudes bring success. When you <u>turn your pity-party into a happy state of mind—ideas, directions, inspirations, and success follow</u>. You cannot sell when you are depressed. Remember, <u>jokes can and will take you and your customers out of bad moments, bad thoughts, and pity-parties</u>.

Johnny Langston

You can overcome any obstacle in your life if you: 1) accept an obstacle for what it is—an obstacle—do not be in denial. 2) plan on how to overcome your obstacle—getting advice or counsel is not a bad idea, and 3) meet your obstacle head-on, go through it, go around it, or jump over it. You cannot overcome your obstacle by avoiding it. You will have to deal with obstacles in one form or another—it may be financial, emotional, physical or mental—but there is an obstacle with your name on it.

Let me introduce you to my contractor Johnny Langston. If you do not understand anything I have said, please understand this one thing. Johnny Langston and I built hundreds of homes. We developed subdivisions. We built the Brown Construction Company office building directly across the street, in front of A & T College which is a university now.

I used to drive up to the Brown Construction Company every morning, looking over at A & T College waving my "C" and "D" transcript – all the while I was making hundreds of thousands of dollars! If I can do it this way, you can too! <u>Do not allow your personal failures to hinder your progress</u>. Do not allow your issues to get in your way.

I had to encourage myself. When no one out there encourages you, know this: <u>you must depend on yourself for encouragement. You've got to encourage yourself, when no one else will.</u>

Johnny and I worked together in peace and love seven days a week. You have to let go of old prejudices. You have to look past race, economics, color, ethnicity, sexual preference, gender, age, disability or the lack thereof and see everything and everyone as an opportunity for them to benefit from what you have to offer. That's the way you get "big time," by coming together. This is what took place.

I was at my peak as a builder. One of my competitors filed a complaint against me, which read: "You are building out of your price range." My license only covered me to build homes up to $80,000 in value. A client who was a doctor persuaded me to build his home. This home would be valued at about $300,000. I had gotten the home halfway finished; when the state department from Raleigh, North Carolina put a big condemned sign on the construction: *"Cease All Construction."*

When you are climbing your ladder of personal success, obstacles and hurdles are guaranteed to come your way. How you handle these delays will mean your success or failure. Be positive in your approach to your obstacles. Learn to overcome your obstacle, realizing that an obstacle is only a stumbling block which you step on or over to get to your prize. No pain, no gain—remember. See your obstacles as opportunities.

Your competitors may become angry, jealous, or bitter towards you because of your success or your potential success. Stay focused on your goals and be determined to reach them. Keep your head up as you climb your ladder to your personal success so, that you can see anything negative, which may fall your way. In addition, be mindful of those below you who may attempt to bring you down—but your main focus is your sales goals, your customers' benefits, and referrals.

In order to get a license to build homes in the $300,000 price range, I had to take an exam and pass. It was a test on construction, which was loaded with mathematics. AC Brown who has struggled with mathematics all of his life, now has a challenge. I had a real challenge. I had to go to Raleigh, North Carolina and take a math test of 125 problems – which included estimating lumber and other materials. Now that was a real challenge for me. I had to stay focused on my goals. I had to do what was necessary to attain my goals. I dreamed about being that big time developer and here was my opportunity to move up to the next level in the home building business.

I was determined to pass this test. I was not going to allow this test to hold me back nor turn me around. <u>Suppose you and I would approach each and every situation in our lives with the determination that we are going to win</u>. Create the discipline you need during tough times by practicing that type of discipline in good times. How can I do this you may ask?

Practice positive expectations. Practice perseverance. Change your expectations. Practice focusing and spending time working on and working your goals. <u>Practice not only</u>

talking the talk of success, but live the life style of the successful by practicing successful personality traits. Put your heart into what you are doing. Put your nose to the grindstone. Press your foot down on the accelerator and get moving in your sales. The success of so many people lies dormant within them. Unlock your potential.

In my heart, I knew that if both Johnny and I took the test, one of us would pass it. Johnny and I studied together at night after work. We had two weeks to get ready. I learned more about Johnny Langston in those two weeks than I had known for a period of twelve years. We studied at his home. Johnny would put on a pot of coffee and we would sit there until 1 or 2 am in the morning. Oh, I knew we had the exam in the bag because Johnny Langston could figure building materials so close he could put the leftovers in the trunk of his automobile. But I didn't know about AC Brown.

Work Together In Unity

Monday morning we headed to Raleigh, North Carolina to take the exam. We were ready. The instructor passed us the test papers and we began. Johnny's telephone rang. His wife had become seriously ill.

Well, I had to do it—I had to pass this test. I sat there spellbound for about eight minutes. Then I began reading the problems. The answers started coming to me like snowflakes falling from the sky. The answers, the procedures, how to work those math problems came as fast as I could write. I could not believe what was happening to me. This was all I needed to pass this exam. My expectation and determination were coming to fruition.

When I finished taking that examination, the instructor said, "Mr. Brown, since you're here, let me grade your paper."

"Why not?"

The instructor finished grading my paper and he said, "Mr. Brown, why haven't you been here before?"

"I didn't need to come before," I replied, "I came when I had to come."

He said, "You can figure building materials so close, you can put the leftovers in the trunk of an automobile."

I felt great walking out of that exam room. It is great when you accomplish your goals and objectives. That is why it is important <u>to be totally committed and work uncompromisingly on your goals</u>.

Home Builders Association

Through persistence, determination, and hard work, I became a member of the Home Builders Association in Greensboro, NC. I was one of the newest builders in the organization. Now, I was competing with all the other contractors in Greensboro in my home building price range for business opportunities. Then I entered the annual "Parade of Homes" contest where hundreds of more experienced builders were competing for top honors. But remember this always, through God, all things are possible for him that believes.

My very first year as a member, Brown Construction and Realty won the "Parade of Homes" contest. Remember, we were competing with hundreds of builders. Thousands of people from all over the entire state of North Carolina toured the home which the Brown Construction Company built. And guess who drew the plans? My wife, Gladys Lea Ruffin Brown.

In fact, Gladys drew all the plans that the Brown Construction and Realty Company built – including elevations and plot plans.

<u>Read this book daily</u>. <u>Do "Your Daily Affirmations"</u> daily. Over and over, and over again, remembering that repetition is a wonderful thing. Then go out there and execute the business acumen which you have developed.

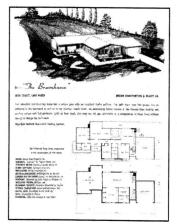

<u>Go out there and apply what you have learned</u>. Apply it again and again. Do it, then do it and do it again. As long as you just sit and sit and sit and read and read and read and don't attempt to apply it and attempt to apply it again; you will never, never, never get the success, which you desire. When you finish this book, read it again and tell a friend to purchase a copy also.

☙ ❧

Week 4 – My Daily Sales Affirmations

1. I will practice having a desire for success.
2. I will apply the procedures that work and make better choices concerning my sales goals.
3. I will practice not having a pity-party but keep a happy state of mind.
4. I realize that jokes can and will take my customers and me out of bad moments, bad thoughts, and pity-parties.
5. I will not allow my personal failures to hinder my progress.
6. I will depend on myself for encouragement. I will encourage myself, when no one else will.
7. I will approach every situation in my life with the determination that I am going to win.
8. I will practice not only talking the talk of success, but live the lifestyle of the successful by practicing successful personality traits.
9. I believe that through God, all things are possible. I will believe it and practice it.
10. I will apply what I have learned in life to my sales approaches and closes.

(Proven Techniques from AC Brown's 48-Year Track Record)

CHAPTER

5

Walking
Into a Setup

෩   ෬

Chapter 5

Walking Into a Setup

Arriving in Atlanta

I want you to think here for a moment. I want you to do some serious thinking here. Just think about this one thing. In about every home across this land, there are one, two, or there could be three slow learners. They just can't get it together. When they understand the principles I teach here, their lives are going to take on a new meaning.

This book is a great gift for the youth in your household. This will give them the tools they need to be successful in life without being "the sharpest knife in the drawer." Share this book with them and encourage them to stick with it.

I left Greensboro, North Carolina arriving in Atlanta, Georgia thinking I was there to build houses, sub-divisions and apartment community homes. I even organized the Medallion Construction Company for this purpose. I could not get the building business off the ground because of lack of finances. Everything was all tied up in a Real Estate development deal in Greensboro, which positioned me in Atlanta in a "starting over" mode with little cash flow and a family to feed.

This is what happened in Greensboro, North Carolina before I moved to Atlanta. I had built a sub-division development without using Federal Home Administration (FHA) guidelines. Because the homes in the sub-division did not meet FHA bank loan requirements, prospective purchasers could not afford the large down payments required by the banks. Our prospective residents would have to make a down payment of 10 to 20% in order to get their loans approved. We could not find prospective buyers with the cash reserves of 10 to 20% of the sale prices. As a result, the vacant homes just set there as interest continued to accrue.

Here, I found out quickly that building single-family homes, apartment community homes, or sub-divisions, was Herman Russell's territory. He was a well-known and established builder in Atlanta. No one was interested in talking to a new starter upper without finances. At this time, my mind was set on building. I had done so well in the construction business, until I got stuck with the subdivision mentioned earlier. When I arrived in Atlanta, my focus was on providing for my family, so naturally I fell back on what I had done in the past to be successful.

I soon discovered that I had to make a change. Building was out of the question. I asked God for an answer. The answer came to me. "Sell other peoples houses." Well, I thought, *"That means getting a Real Estate license, salesmanship skills, and the whole nine yards."* I developed a mindset for success in this new venture. I was determined to master this change. If I did it, you can too. I passed the real estate exam, studying every chance I could get. I read books, listened to audio tapes, CD's and attended seminars. Oh, you have to got to mean business and prepare for the assignment.

Getting into Real Estate

I got my Real Estate license very quickly. The first home that I closed, I made a commission of only $100. Because of his concern, my Real Estate broker, Lonnie Fuller on Hunter Street, called my wife and me into his office.

Lonnie said, "Mr. Brown, you need to let your wife become qualified to teach here. You've got two sons you've got to take care of." He continued, "Real Estate is tough here. Your family can live on her income as a teacher while you learn how to sell Real Estate."

This was during the time of "white flight" in Atlanta neighborhoods. He said that we should co-op with Stovall, a Caucasian Real Estate broker; because being African-American, I could not knock on Caucasian doors soliciting listings. This meant that I would be selling Stovall's listings and splitting commissions.

"Please," he went on, "do not go to Cascade Heights and try to list properties. They'll lynch you over there. We just had a barricade here."

He was correct. A barricade had been erected in the Cascade Heights neighborhood to keep blacks out. I excused myself to go to the water fountain. I didn't need a drink of water, I was really <u>getting to a more quiet location so I could think more clearly</u>. I was going to move in on the Cascade Heights neighborhood and sell like crazy ignoring those prejudiced folk who saw only black and white, while I was seeing green. I wasn't going to put up a sign until I got a whole street of houses sold.

This is your day. Live life loving it! Get involved, join life. <u>Make a benefit-centered decision</u>. <u>Stop being a passive observer in life and be an active participant.</u> Do it the way I teach you and success will be yours. When I went up with a whole street of signs I didn't hear the name Stovall mentioned again. Lonnie sat back and counted the commission checks.

Every day we are going through a training program, which is preparing us for the next level. When you remember you are in training, your mistakes and failures affect you less negatively because you understand that you are in a life-long training program, which ends when you die. Poor decisions and failures along with good decisions and successes are a part of every human life.

Frank Ward was my loan officer and Patsy Ward, his wife was the mortgage processor. They were our team members who worked with the mortgage broker. They worked together with us to move hundreds of homes. At that time, white people wanted to move out of Cascade Heights and East Point. They wanted out of West End, Sewell Road (Benjamin E. Mays Drive), Audubon Forest, Campbellton Road, and Beecher Road, to name a few. They would pay off the car notes of buyers. They would pay off furniture notes for the buyer and in some cases the fleeing whites would leave their furniture in the house, in an effort to get out of the area as soon as possible, even though there were only a few blacks living in their neighborhoods at the time. Remember, they had only recently had a barricade on Cascade Road to keep blacks out.

The Wards and my wife and I had synergy and compatibility of effort in assisting the highly motivated whites who wanted to move before the blacks took over their neighborhood, though few blacks lived there. The Wards brought something to the table and so did we. We have to think about what our contributions are when we are working with others. You do not want to come to the table empty-handed. Do your best to contribute as much as possible.

We invited Frank and Patsy Ward to dinner one night. The appointment was for seven o'clock. We were on time and they had not arrived at the designated time. My wife and I sat there. After waiting thirty minutes, we placed our order. We had just about finished eating when I saw them coming in, walking very fast. I stood up. <u>When you take action and take that first step, spontaneity will be working for you.</u> I did not know what I was going to say when I stood up.

"Frank," I said, "you and Patsy have hung out with us so much you have stolen our bad habit of being late." We all laughed as we sat and thoroughly enjoyed dinner and conversation together.

From that day, for a period of twenty some years, we developed an outstanding working relationship together. We started going out together on weekends. We even joined the Skylark Club in Atlanta, and we flew all over America once a month—getting on airplanes without knowing the destinations until we arrived.

Boy, was that a lot of fun. We didn't just party on these trips—no! We studied financing together, talked strategies, practiced techniques and smoothed out as many rough places in our programs as possible.

Working on the weekends during those trips would prepare us for progress upon arriving back at the office

Monday morning to work. You will be surprised at what happens when you come together in preparation with the people with whom you work.

You will be surprised at what happens when you work together with your fellow human beings. It is a little, big thing called synergism. <u>Two minds are better than one</u>. The sum of the whole is greater than any of the parts. You may have heard these truisms.

Come Together to Create Synergy

If Frank Ward got a rejection on one of my Real Estate cases, I was Frank's backup. We would sit down just like two medical doctors discussing a patient's case together. We lost very few Real Estate transactions. If I can do it this way, you can too! <u>Come together to create synergism!</u>

However, you have to come together at least five days a week with your team members to create synergism. I remember one night we were flying into Atlanta from Las Vegas. We were having a lot of fun on that plane. A Caucasian brother looked back and asked Frank, "Are you people related to one another?" Frank looked at me and pointed, "That's my brother!"

So don't you be afraid to do what I am imparting into you concerning building your wealth; both your spiritual wealth and your personal wealth.

༺ ༻

Hightower Road Apartments

Hightower Road Apartments. This is an example of how success can be yours if you persevere and work hard while believing you can do it. <u>It can pay off for you as you work your business goals, sales goals, and personal goals</u>. Success doesn't just happen; it doesn't just fall into your hands. You have to do some things, drill through your mountains, maneuver your resources, and swim your oceans. Do not stop nor give up. It is not about being in the right place at the right time; <u>it is about placing yourself at the right place at the right time with the right words, and the right people</u>.

This is an example of how ingenuity, the right sales techniques—using the correct approaches, using the most prodigious sales presentations and closes worked for me to develop Hightower Road Apartments which Metropolitan

Atlanta Rapid Transit Authority (MARTA) condemned for its "right of way" and how what I learned and how I executed what I learned can work for you.

I was in my office on Lynhurst Drive, selling 10-15 homes were month. I was the sole salesperson involved in presenting these home sales opportunities to prospective buyers and sellers; no one else was involved in my sales. To this day, I don't know how in the world I did it all but by the Grace of God, I did it. Dealing with this much diversified property management requires detailed planning, organization, and the power of focus.

This is how it all happened. One day, while sitting in my office, a man walked in. Oh, this man could sell; and he was dressed for the occasion. Listen to what this man said to me.

After introducing himself, he said, "Mr. Brown, I have a great investment for you. There is this vacant plot of land that will be condemned by MARTA in two years. You can get it at a good price now and make a great profit upon MARTA's condemnation."

Boy, did he have my attention. Every Real Estate man wants a huge profit on an investment. This sounded like one of those transactions to me. It seemed too good to be true. You know we can talk too much and talk ourselves out of a sale. Sometimes it pays to listen. This man had my attention; I was listening.

He said, "The price is right. $100,000."

You know what they say, *"If it looks like it's too good to be true—then it most likely is."*

"This plot consists of three acres located on Hightower Road and you can have it for a measly $100,000. The good thing about this, it is zoned for apartments."

He didn't have to say anything else. However, there is one thing I want to point out to everyone who reads this book. I acted as if I did not know anything about MARTA coming through the area—specifically, right through that property. I knew it already because people had been talking about MARTA coming through.

Immediately after this man left, I carried the good news home to my family. My house filled with the joy of the money I expected to make from my tenants who would live there for two to three years, and from the money that I would make when paid by MARTA upon the condemnation of the property.

My two sons ran around the house singing this song, *"Daddy is going to make a whole lot of money. Daddy is going to make a whole lot of money."*

I heard my wife tell my oldest son this, "Your daddy is a very smart businessman."

I even thought so myself until I got to city hall to get the building permit. That is when I discovered that I had bought a piece of land which I had put $100,000 into, money dispersed and the transaction closed, only to discover that there was no way to bring in water nor sewer onto the property.

I discovered that Herman Russell and all the big time Real Estate men had refused to deal with those three acres on Hightower Road for this reason—there was no way to have access to water or sewer.

"Oh that Tim got you didn't he Mr. Brown?" That is what the man at city hall who was selling the building permits said to me.

He was referring to Tim Alexander who sold me the property. I could have frozen at this time. <u>You can think you are making a mistake, but don't</u>. Your family may think you are making a mistake, but don't you think that way. <u>Think positively and expect positive results.</u> These sales techniques can turn a fortune. I did not fall into a pity-party. <u>Don't you ever fall into a pity-party</u>. Count everything that comes your way as joy.

> "My brethren, count it all joy when ye fall into divers temptations; knowing *this*, that the trying of your faith worketh patience. But let patience have

her perfect work, that ye may be perfect and entire, <u>wanting nothing</u>." James 1:2-4 (KJV)

This thing which looked like a "pity-party" at first, turned out to be a three-fold blessing. If I had not persevered, believing what the Creator has promised, working my sales techniques, the purchase of that property would have truly been a lemon. But you see <u>with hard work and faith in myself and in the process that I was using, success was not far away</u>. You must keep working at it.

Life can be a struggle sometimes and during this period in my life, it was tough. <u>When life gets tough, so do you— you get equally tough. You will be rewarded if only you keep on pushing.</u> Like I said, it was tough and I had to believe every step of the way; no matter how bad the situation looks, no matter how deep the trouble, you and I must push on.

I had the property surveyed and a design by the engineer brought water and sewer from Burton Road to my property. Having solved this problem, I had plans drawn for the apartment home community and finally the loan was approved. Construction commenced and the site had to be overseen and managed. Remember, <u>what may look like an impossibility, is only a blessing in disguise</u>.

The Hightower Road apartment home community was finally completed. We filled the rental units using marketing and sales techniques in the newspaper and on the telephone. During this time, my duties and responsibilities consisted of:

1) Selling 10-15 houses per month, 2) Dealing with the water department telling me I had no water nor sewer rights on the land I had just purchased; the land being the old City Dump, 3) Supervising the manager of our Cascade Cabana Apartments which we owned and managed, 4) Dealing with the Surveyor shooting from Burton Road, 5) And eventually dealing with the property salesman who sold me the property to which water and sewer rights were finally granted, trying to buy the land back from me for double the price.

Two years later in comes MARTA, condemning properties left and right in metro Atlanta—pushing the public transportation issue right through this property, which now has a 60-unit apartment home community sitting on it.

Now guess what? MARTA only wanted to pay us a penance for the property. It seems that people were not getting what their property was worth unless they had good legal help. I knew I needed an attorney to help me fight MARTA for my rights. And that is just what I got from J.

Kenneth Lee, an attorney from North Carolina. I contacted J. Kenneth Lee. I told him that I needed his services but I did not have any money to pay him.

"Brown, pay me when you get it," is what J. Kenneth Lee said to me. Just send me all the paperwork and correspondence that you receive.

I was sending J. Kenneth Lee documentations everyday. So I sent him everything that I receive from MARTA and the city of Atlanta. And I do mean everything. Kenneth evaluated all of the correspondence and discovered that MARTA was not following Federal guidelines, State guidelines, nor their own guidelines. MARTA was doing condemnations in a manner that was beneficial to MARTA.

I paid for his ticket to come to Atlanta, Georgia to represent me in court against MARTA. J. Kenneth Lee had to file a brief before going to court. He called the judge before coming to Atlanta. Guess what he said to the judge?

"I am not coming down there just to argue procedure," Kenneth Lee told the judge, "I am coming down there to close MARTA down. I have documentation to prove that they have not followed federal, state, nor city guidelines." Kenneth Lee continued, "And your Honor, tell them if I do not win this case in Atlanta, I will win it in Washington, D.C. I am coming down there to shut MARTA down if they do not do the right thing in this case."

Do you know that they would not go to court with Kenneth? We settled through arbitration. This is a beautiful world in which we are living. You have to know how to use these sales techniques to get your personal success. You cannot lose with these proven techniques. If I can do it, you can too. Learn these good sales approaches and techniques; then persevere to accomplishment.

☙ ❧

Week 5–My Daily Sales Affirmations

1. From now on, when I make a decision, I will be more serious about it and follow through with it.
2. When I need more clarity concerning an issue, I will go to a quiet location so I can think more clearly.
3. I will make benefit-centered decisions for my customers and myself.
4. I will stop being a passive observer in life and become an active participant.
5. I will come together with my sales team to create synergy!
6. I will focus my attention on my business goals, my sales goals, and my personal goals.
7. I will practice placing myself at the right place at the right time with the right words.
8. When making a decision, I will not think for a second that I am making a mistake.
9. I will practice thinking positively and expecting positive results.
10. When life gets tough, so will I. I will get equally tough and persevere.
11. I will keep pushing towards my goals, while expecting positive results.

(Proven Techniques from AC Brown's 48-Year Track Record)

CHAPTER 6

Words for the Wise

Chapter 6

Words for the Wise

Use Intelligent Key Words and Statements

This chapter is from an article AC submitted to Real Estate Today, an organization of over 300,000 Realtors. Study each of these techniques carefully and apply as many of them as you can to whatever you are selling or plan to sell.

When you're working with buyers and sellers, <u>the intelligent selection of key words and statements is imperative</u> in establishing and maintaining the positive mental attitude that is an essential element in making the sale. Often it's a simple matter which words are the best to use for a particular situation and then using these words.

<u>We must realize which words are the best to use for a particular situation. We then use this knowledge for an expected measured result in conversation and action from your prospective customers.</u>

Here are some prime examples of words and statements that we encounter every day.

1. <u>Never say, "I'm calling to confirm our appointment.</u>" You can accomplish this purpose without using those words, which might insult the person's competence to keep his appointment. If he already had any doubt about keeping that date, you just offered him or her the perfect way out.

<u>When you call to confirm an appointment to demonstrate your product, try this approach.</u>

"*Mrs. Adams*, this is Joe Jones. I have selected the perfect setup, home, or product, whatever the case may be, for your business. Then give a clear brief description. Example: I have selected the perfect home for you and your family. It has a large separate dining room that will accommodate all of your furniture and a beautiful spacious kitchen with all of the latest conveniences. I'm looking forward to seeing you today at 10:00 a.m. Be sure to bring the children along. I know they will find the fenced-in yard and swing set a lot of fun."

<u>Also ask to speak to the spouse and address his interests.</u>

"*Mr. Adams*, I've selected the perfect home for you and your family. It has a large modern kitchen that your wife wants and a wonderful yard for children. It also has a full basement for your workshop and a nicely paneled den that could serve as your office. Note how this approach appeals to all members of the family."

2. <u>Never use the words "qualify" or "afford."</u> These are words to use with professionals. They can make prospective buyers defensive and apprehensive. Your prospective buyers do not want you to tell them what they can and cannot afford. Your questions will determine their level of affordability.

3. <u>Say "agreement," not "contract."</u> Buyers want to feel that they are entering freely into a transaction, not that they are obligated against their will.

4. <u>Say "initial investment," not "down payment."</u> The term "down payment" implies that this is just the tip

of the iceberg of payments to come. Do not give buyers unnecessary opportunities to worry about future payments. "Initial investment," on the other hand, conveys the idea that an intelligent business transaction is taking place. Everyone wants and needs reinforcement that he is making a good decision. This phrase also brings to mind the idea of a return of one's investment. Such little differences in wording can make the big difference between a close and a no-close.

5. Before showing your product, <u>never say, "Lets go look.</u>" Say instead, "Let's select." If you say, "Look," that is exactly what the prospects are going to do. "Select" is really what you want them to do, isn't it?

6. <u>Never think, "I'm going to show this product."</u> Think, "I'm going to sell this product." You must program yourself to close sales.

7. <u>Say, "We want to arrange for financing;" not "We want a credit application</u>." Often the word credit reminds prospective buyers of past financial experiences that they think may cause problems. Hence, to avoid facing reality, they will give excuses for not buying. In actuality, these financial

experiences may not adversely affect the prospect's ability to buy at all.

8. <u>When you're talking about price, leave off the thousands and dollars.</u> Try saying, "Mr. Adams, the price is 70." He will still understand you, but 70 sounds less intimidating than $70,000.

9. <u>Never say, "deal"; always use "transaction."</u> The word "deal" has a suspicious tone to it; "transaction" has a more legitimate connotation.

10. <u>Say, "I congratulate you" more often than "thank you."</u> Saying "thank you" implies that the prospects have done something for you, whereas, "I congratulate you" confirms the fact that they have made the right decision for themselves.

11. <u>Never say, "You won't be sorry."</u> This is a negative approach. Prospects may begin to think, "Perhaps I will be sorry." A better approach is to say, "You'll be proud of yourselves."

12. <u>Never ask, "Would you like to buy this product.</u> People may think that they have bought too much already. Ask instead, "Would you like an

opportunity to invest in this home or product?"

13. <u>If your product is a house, never say "offer"; say "contract."</u> When you tell the seller that you have an "offer," you are telling him that you have cut the price of his home and that the buyer is just bidding. If you tell the seller that you have a "contract," he feels that you have sold his home. You never want to give the seller the impression that a buyer is just bidding on his asking price.

14. <u>Use colorful, descriptive glamorous words</u>. Imagine a sandwich made with thinly sliced, sweet Danish ham; aged Swiss cheese; fresh, crisp Iceberg lettuce; and sliced firm, ripe tomatoes on freshly baked cracked wheat bread. Doesn't that sound a lot more appetizing than ham and cheese on whole wheat? In the same manner, you can make that "ham-and-cheese" product called real estate or what ever it is you are selling, sound a lot more appealing to your prospective c.

Study, Rehearse Approach, Close

Study. Know. Rehearse. Approach. Close. Succeed. Study your market and product. Know your sales approach. Rehearse your presentation. Engage your potential client, using the professional sales approaches and sales closes I am sharing with you and success will be yours.

Do not always stay on the beaten path; try something different. It is often said, *"Insanity is doing things the same way and expecting a different result."* Try something new.

Make your goals a part of your personality. Remember, some things you can only do if you own your own business. Some risks you can only take if you own your own business.

Success is
Preparation
Connecting with
Opportunity

When you work for others, you must follow their rules, which may not relate to selling the way you would do it if you were working for yourself.

Do not allow fear to turn you off and on. Do not let fear turn you off of a proposal, a business transaction, a way of life or off your sales goals. Stick with your plan—your goals.

Place your goals where you can see them daily—a refrigerator will do just fine. Do you have a plan? Do you live your plan? Here comes the wife. Are you going to stick to the plan? Here comes decision time. Here comes your child; its decision time. Here comes the husband; its decision time. Are you going to stick to your goals? Here comes your boss. Are you going to stick to the plan—to your goals?

I made the decision and I have to deal with the consequences of the decision. I am going to make the decision happen; goal by goal, step by step, day by day, systematically. <u>Write it down and make it simple and place it on your refrigerator, reviewing it everyday</u>. If I can do it this way, you can too!

<u>We are talking sales approaches and closes here</u>. Is this your decision or your wife's decision? Is this your decision or your husband's decision? Is this a decision made for a child? Is it your decision or your boss's decision? Is this your decision or your prospective customer's decision? You are the boss of you -- are you operating this way? Are you making your decisions and following them?

We all should look at it this way; there is a _plan, a purpose for every individual who is alive on this earth_. This kind of language is easy to say, but not easy to believe, and certainly not easy to live for most individuals. You must believe from the top of your head to the bottom of your feet that you will be successful in your personal and business endeavors. This will activate and energize you to accomplish your daily sales goals. _There is a chasm between doing the successful things in your life and believing that you can do the successful things that can be done in your life_. Bridge that chasm.

                                      ℘   ☙

I have been into several fields and made millions in each field. My success has been the result of hard work. You can imagine my excitement right about now. _When you believe that that something is for you and you expect it with all your heart, believing without a doubt and it doesn't happen—do not get into a pity-party_. You are looking in the face of a blessing delayed; one which is being multiplied on your behalf. _Give it time to multiply and get back to you_.

Your day is coming. So _you have to prepare_ for it. Our trip through this land is _preparation meeting opportunity_. _Our successful trip through this land is knowledge_ prepared to meet opportunity. You have the equipment. Let me show you how to use it. Apply what you learn from this book. When you do it the way I teach you, the bricks automatically fall into place as if magic hands are placing them there. If you have prepared, it is going to happen.

❧ ☙

Week 6–My Daily Sales Affirmations

1. I will select and use intelligent key words and statements and maintain a positive mental attitude.
2. I will consciously consider which words are the best to use for a particular situation.
3. I will use the correct words to attain the expected result in conversations and actions.
4. I will study my market and know my product. I will know my sales presentation and rehearse it.
5. I will not always stay on the beaten path, but will attempt different approaches.
6. I will make my goals a part of my personality.
7. I will not allow fear to turn me off nor on.
8. I will write down my goals; and place them on my refrigerator, reviewing it daily.
9. There is a plan and a purpose for my life. If I do not have a plan, I will make one now and follow it.

(Proven Techniques from AC Brown's 48-Year Track Record)

CHAPTER 7

Sales Approach Insights

Chapter 7

Sales Approach Insights

Professional Approaches

Adapt these techniques of professional sales approaches to your specific business. Consider the possibilities for your business and the potential for increasing your sales opportunities as you read the following paragraphs on professional sales approaches. Imagine how you can integrate these professional sales approaches into the type of business you have or where you work. Apply them to your daily work experience, and remember—<u>practice, practice, practice</u>.

This chapter is about effective sales approaches, how they work, and how to implement them into your daily sales experience. The major principle to know about sales approaches is you have to practice them daily until they become a part of you. You must practice speaking them in every sales situation over and over again until they become a part of your personality.

I am going to say this for what it is worth, regardless of what you do for a living, the approach is necessary; it is a must. Successful approaches lead to closings. <u>You must know what, when, and how to say it</u> in order to get your prospect to do what you want them to do without confusing or irritating them. Once you learn the approach and know why the approach is necessary, then you can close, using the appropriate closing approach.

Let me share this experience with you. As I was fine-tuning my sales approaches as a young salesperson, I would practice my approaches on anyone and everyone, no matter the location, the venue, the time or day or night or the occupation, class or color of the person standing in front of me. I wanted to sell "big-time" so I knew that I had to practice my approaches until the approaches turned to closes.

One day I was in an apartment home community waiting for someone for a meeting. There was a little girl playing in the parking area. What did I do? You guessed it.

I went up to her just as bold and asked, "Little girl do you want to move into a brand new home?"

She looked at me with wonder in her eyes, "Mister," she said, "I am not supposed to talk to strangers, and I am not old enough to buy a house. I don't have a job, but I heard my mom and dad the other night talking about buying a house."

Wasn't I amazed? Here I was just practicing for my potential customer who had yet to arrive and here is this young lady talking about her parents desiring to purchase a house. I gave her my business card and told her to take it immediately to her parents or to give it to them when they arrived home.

I told her, "Let your parents know that I think you are a smart little girl and that when you get older, I will give you a job working with me in my real estate company."

Practice Selling and Upselling

She went on her way and so did I, watching her to see where she lived so I could go back and give a more polished sales approach to her parents. Practice is important in every field of endeavor, especially in sales; whether you are selling or upselling; upselling hamburgers or chicken at a fast food restaurant, selling retail, wholesale, automobiles, apartment homes or real estate; practice is the key to your sales' success.

Selling Anything and Everything

This is how to sell anything and everything: you start your approach with the closing in mind. I just gave you a million dollars worth of sales experience in this one statement. Now listen carefully, I am going to talk to you as though you are a seasoned sales professional who knows your product and knows the benefits that your product has to offer your customer.

1. You see the person in front of you, <u>not as a "potential" customer, but as a "satisfied" customer</u>. This one idea changes the dynamic in your relationship to the person standing in front of you. This is a positive approach. You cannot be successful in sales unless you <u>take a positive approach</u>. Be positive in your attire. Be positive in your conversation. Be positive about everything you see, say, or do.

You may be experiencing an earthquake, but *"that earthquake sure help settle the food in my stomach."* Be extremely positive about everything and if the "sold" customer has negative things to say, find something positive to say about the issue or find another issue. Agreement has the potential to help your sale, but changing the subject to another one, which is more positive, helps to move your sale along to the positive closing you desire. A negative conversation where agreement is engaged may continue the negativity to a no close, which you do not want. You can always change their basis of thinking. Remember, you are in charge. <u>You must direct the conversation</u>.

2. <u>You must be energetic</u>. When you walk, you walk as though you have somewhere to go, someone to meet, and that you are the top salesperson in your company. (You have to act as if you going to sell something. Moreover, chances are you will.) Hold your head high and your shoulders back. If you believe you are the top salesperson in the company and work at it, soon you may become that person. Know that

hard work does not escape anyone who wants to get to the top in their field of endeavor.

3. <u>You approach your prospect as though he is your "long lost" high school best buddy</u>. You have missed seeing him. You ask about his family, relatives, and friends. You want to know where the children are and what grades they are in in school; what university they are attending or which ones they want to attend.

You let them know your educational background and let them know if there is any way you can assist them with helping their children get into that "first choice" school to let you know how you can help. You are truly sincere in these requests and suggestions, even though you may never have an opportunity to assist them. However, your "sold" customer knows that you asked, and the "asking" says to them you are interested in them. This leads us to number four.

4. <u>Take a real and sincere personal interest in the persons standing in front of you</u>. Truly think about how you can help them. How do you show the persons standing or sitting in front of you

that you have a sincere interest in them? Your eyes are locked onto their eyes when they talk and when you talk. Attempt to spend as much eye time as possible connecting your eyes with theirs. Now, do not blink when you look at them. To some people, blinking means you are lying, and you are not doing that.

<u>You know your product will benefit them</u>. They may know your product will benefit them, but if you offer assistance in the areas of their lives which needs some assistance and is the focus of their lives, they will be willing to give you more of their "mind" space for receiving whatever it is you have to say. Remember, you must be sincere in your words and know this may require following up those words with actions. This leads to...

5. Unconscious prospecting or referrals. When you use this technique you get the "sold" customer to tell their neighbors, relatives and friends about this nice young man or that nice lady that helped them in some way or another. They are now including you in their daily conversations with their inner circles.

Now you have to know this is going to happen, so it is important for you to give them words and phrases which are easy for them to remember about you or your product. For example: Let's say your name is Alonza Cassie Brown. You do not leave them with the name, Mr. Brown nor Mr. Alonza. You let them take with them, "AC." That is a friendly name, easy to remember and is disarming.

6. Disarm your prospect. How do you disarm the person standing in front of you? The number one way to do this is to smile. You must have a smile in your heart and sincerity on your lips. The key to disarming a person is to use positive physical, physiological, emotional, and life circumstance attributes which are shared with others, i.e., smiles, jokes, laughter, encouragement, hope, potential, and other positive re-enforcements.

My greatest positive re-enforcements which were very successful for me were: a) jokes, and b) smiling while talking. Your jokes must be clean in nature and easy to say, not very long, and easy to remember. Why? Because your customer is going to tell that joke to your next customer, i.e., their neighbors, relatives, and friends. This will help your new prospects know about you before they get a chance to see you.

7. <u>You are my number one customer</u>. Or you are the only customer that I have. This my friend is attitude. When you display this attitude to your customers as if they are the only customer you have, or the number one customer you have, what happens is you transform yourself into the number one salesperson in your field. This state of mind also transforms your customer into one who is more likely to be loyal to you and your business and who is willing to support your efforts when they may not be truly interested in doing so. You will find that when you treat your customers, i.e., that one customer which is standing or sitting across from you, like they are the only friend you have, they will stop and listen to everything you have to say because you will truly be exhibiting a keen sense of interest in him.

8. <u>Stop, reflect, and evaluate your day</u>. Do not get too busy to stop at the end of your day and reflect on the events and conversations of the day to evaluate what you did right or wrong. Take a moment from the television news and the newspaper and those negative current events and meditate on your day in a quiet, peaceful location, like by a stream or creek; while walking down a wooded path; swinging on an adult swing set at the neighborhood playground; or listening to the rain in the arboretum.

Make the location an exterior one and set the activity level at a minimum; you want to be able to pull out your note pad and write down your reflections so you do not have to remember them when you get back home or back to the office. If you practice writing down your reflections, you will find that you will receive more of them as you will create brain space for more reflections by not having to remember them. Try this, it works wonders for building your business acumen, sales potential, and personal life successes. Listen to the birds singing, while you are at it.

Automobile Selling

P**rofessional Automobile Selling.** Here is the professional approach I have used over the course of my 48-year record of accomplishment to sell any product or service. This is how you can sell a large number of automobiles. Let's say you have 200 cars out there on the automobile dealership lot. Here comes this one couple walking in, and they only want one automobile and there are 200 automobiles in your lot. Just think. They are on your lot. Now remember, they saw those 200 automobiles before they got to you. Another thing to note is that <u>they have come to your automobile dealership, not someone else's dealership</u>.

And now, how do you go about making the sale to this one couple? Remember, they are only going to purchase one automobile. As a sales person, when they walk into your office you have to size them up quickly. How do you do that? By asking them a series of questions. You do not ask this couple a lot of questions – <u>you only ask pertinent questions, which you know will lead to a sale</u>.

First, ask questions that are of interest to them. How many people are in your family? What family members will be using the car? How long have you had your present car? Why do you want to change? Is color important to you? What features do you want this time?

<u>Do not get into unrelated conversations</u>. You may irritate a buyer and you will get your buyer talking about things that they don't need to be thinking about at this time. Their focus needs to be on the product, which they came into your office to get. See, we have to think that way. You have to know what you are saying. Remember, you are the only one capable of doing it while you have a captive audience. <u>Always frame your questions around the product or service that you are selling</u>.

Those people came to a professional. That is what they expect. Moreover, drop a few words in your presentation to make them laugh, remember laughter creates sales. You sit there very attentively, sliding to the edge of your chair, focusing on their eyes and listening to what they are saying that they want. Once they tell you what you know they want, you compare that with the best product or service that you have that fits their description.

Every professional has to know his or her inventory. That is a must! Now is the time that you jump up and snap your fingers.

You say with a sparkle in your eyes, "I got it."

<u>In one smooth movement, you act as if the perfect product has just been brought to your attention.</u> And they are going to say, or they will be thinking, this man knows what he is doing. They are now focused on you. <u>Their focus is no longer on the product, but on you.</u> You say to the couple, if the product is an automobile, "Come let us go look at your automobile."

> **Speak with Enthusiasm and Excitement**

You walk with energy, as you go to that automobile. Ensure that this automobile is clean and shiny; the interior is clean and the tires are sparkling. But you don't open the door. Just as you go to open the car door, you turn around and look at your potential purchasers, especially the one that acts like he or she is in charge.

You say, "Mr. West, don't you just love this automobile."

Now listen to who says "yes" first. You size up the dominant buyer again. And in a verified tone, look, him in the eyes, and say.

"You will really enjoy this automobile." "Don't you just love it? Don't you just love that new car smell? I can see you riding to your friend's house in it right now!"

Now, they are focused on the automobile, so stay animated. Speak with enthusiasm and excitement. When you see the acknowledgement in their body language and in their faces, you let them drive it a few blocks. Upon returning you say, "Let's go back to my office and complete the paper work for your new car."

This procedure is very professional and it really works. We have kissed those 199 automobiles goodbye, and said "hello" to the right one. So you go right into the office with that couple and you close that sale. I guarantee you that you have a sale. When you sit down, in your office, just start filling out the paper work. If they do not stop you, they have bought that car.

That couple only came to purchase one automobile. That is all you talk about is that one automobile. <u>Sow service</u>. Time is of the essence; those people are busy doing a lot of things in their lives and you are busy also. Make a sale and move on to the next one. That is the way selling is done.

You as a sales representative will love your job as you close one sale after another. You will make a lot of sales doing it the way I teach you. Focus on that one product. Focus on that one sale. Focus on that one automobile. And by the way, if you are out there test driving an automobile, ask questions like this, for instance let's say, tomorrow is Sunday.

"Mr. West, which one of you will be driving this car to church tomorrow?"

Listen to who responds first. Remember that person is the one in charge—the dominant buyer. This is powerful information. The next question would be to that person. This is a powerful technique, I just shared with you. When you ask a question, or make a comment, the person who speaks first is the dominant buyer and your next comment or question is directed towards the person. This person will help you close the sale.

Week 7—My Daily Sales Affirmations

1. I will integrate professional sales approaches into my business. I will apply sales approaches daily at work, remembering to—practice and practice.
2. I will not think of my prospects as a "potential" sale, but as a "satisfied" customer.
3. I will take a positive approach knowing I cannot be successful in sales unless I do.
4. I will be positive in all my conversations with my customers.
5. I will be energetic. My energy increases my sales.
6. I will approach my prospects as though they are my "long lost" high school best friends.
7. I will have a real, sincere, and personal interest in the person standing in front of me.
8. I know my product will benefit my prospects.
9. I will give my customers words and phrases, which are easy for them to remember about my product and me.
10. I will treat each person as if he or she is my number one customer.
11. I will stop at the end of the day to reflect on the events and conversations, evaluating what I did right or wrong.

(Proven Techniques from AC Brown's 48-Year Track Record)

CHAPTER
8

Insight on Closing the Sale

Chapter 8

Insight on Closing the Sale

World's Greatest Sales Trainer

J Douglas Edwards taught professional sales closings to salespersons all over the world. He was the top sales closing trainer at the time of my Real Estate ventures. The late J. Douglas Edwards surely could talk some business of selling to you— "closing your sales" business. Remember, everyone is always selling something and J. Douglas Edwards would say, "Once you ask your closing question, that is when you ask the question whose answer confirms the fact the person has bought, the next thing you do is—SHUT UP!" He would continue, "The first person who speaks is the loser."

J. Douglas Edwards' program was one of professional motivation through communication. At the height of his life experience, he was considered by many to be the world's greatest sales trainer; working with sales persons whose earnings were $100,000 and above, teaching sales closing techniques and sales approaches.

One morning in Atlanta, Georgia, I was fortunate to attend one of his seminars. I made up my mind that morning that I was going to have him spend time with my sales organization to help organize and boost sales. I started writing him soon after the seminar asking him to spend some time with my sales team. I wrote him for a period of six months with no reply. Was I disappointed? No. Did I get angry? No. Did I give up? No. Did I keep trying? Yes. <u>Perseverance is the key</u>. When I make a decision, I do not turn back. If you turn back, you are not going to find the success, which you seek.

> When We Take Action The Universe around Us Takes Action

I sent J. Douglas Edwards' secretary a dozen red roses. With the roses I included a note asking him to come to

Atlanta to teach our organization his professional techniques. He called me the next day.

"Any man that knows how to sell like that," J. Douglas Edwards said, "I've got to come and see what he is about."

He told me that his secretary who had worked for him for twenty-six years had never received a gift of roses from anyone requesting an appointment with him. He came to Atlanta, Georgia for AC Brown and his sales team. He brought his son and they stayed an entire week. He put on one of the most elaborate training programs I've ever experienced in my life. *Boy was I in the "big-time" now*, I thought.

I had to invest over $20,000 in gifts for my sales people to be used during J. Douglas' week of training. The training was so intense we had to close the real estate office and go to a hotel that week. We had "jump" sessions every day. "Jumping" out of our seats with the answers to myriad of questions. The correct answers were rewarded by the special gifts purchased earlier.

At dinner that evening, I asked J. Douglas Edwards this question.

"Why aren't my salespeople consistent in their closing?"

You may have asked this same question yourself. This was his answer.

"They don't want what you want." He continued, "They don't want the same thing that you want, Mr. Brown."

I don't know about you, but I don't buy every answer that comes along. I knew from my 48-year track record -- every man, every woman that walks this earth wants exactly what AC Brown wants. We all want happiness and peace of mind, financial security, the best schools for our children, and the list goes on. We want, but we do not know how to get our wants fulfilled. This is why you are reading this book.

J. Douglas Edwards was so impressed that he made me a part of his sales training presentation because I was the first African-American who had ever hired him. He even had me stand during one of his training seminars. In an audience of about 2,000 attendees, there were only a handful of African-Americans there. I thought it was all about me and my ability to achieve. It was not. <u>It is about getting your potential customers to see the benefits in the service or product, which you offer.</u>

I remember during one of his seminars, which I attended, J. Douglas Edwards walked over to me, out of a crowd of over 1,000 attendees.

"Young man," he said, "why are you so damn excited?"

I replied, "I don't know why, I just am."

"How many houses do you sell a month?" he asked.

"Ten to fifteen a month."

"I see why you are so damn happy!" J. Douglas Edwards laughed as he delivered those words.

<u>Relate your sales presentation and close to the personality of the person who will be in front of you.</u> You have to get serious with your sales approach if you want it to become a part of your personality.

Sales approaches and closes do not work and will not work if you have to turn them off and turn them on. <u>Sales approaches and sales closes will not work and do not work if you turn them off and on due to your fear, apprehension, unpreparedness, or lack of confidence.</u>

We may want to do it *this* way or we may want to do it *that* way – but you must do it the way I am teaching you. Before you use them on the person to whom you are selling, you must practice your approaches and closes. You must practice them so that they become a part of your personality. You do not have to do this your entire lifetime, only during the times in your life, for a season when you want to have financial success through high sales volumes. These approaches and closes must become a part of your daily conversation.

Sow Service Harvest Money

Sow service and harvest money. The key here is that a professional salesperson has to get in tune with the customer. They came to you for assistance. You have the professional advice and product to sell them. You have to be sincere about helping them because they are sincere about coming to you for your assistance. It is a sales connection point. The connection point happens when two minds come together mutually and unknowingly to help one another. But in your case, you know, this is what you want to happen; therefore your conversation moves to make the minds come together. And that is the key to selling. You are not out here just to make money. You are here to fill a need with a product or service.

You have to get in tune with the buyer. You have to <u>have that buyer's interests at heart</u>: and this is the key to big-time selling. This is true of real estate selling, automobile selling, apartment home leasing, and any type of product or service. We are supposed to sow service and harvest money, in that order. Find out what their needs are and do everything that you can to satisfy those needs.

If you are an automobile salesperson, sit down and allow your customer to give you a vivid description of the automobile that he desires, including exterior, interior, and features. Make sure, you, the professional automobile salesperson, sit on the edge of your seat, look them in the eyes, and hear exactly what they are saying to you. Get them laughing as you listen. Your production will rise so fast, you will not believe it.

A more laid-back approach is: lean back in your chair confidently, cross your legs and asked them with self-assurance to describe the car they want to drive out of the car dealership. What you are trying to project is that you are extremely confident that your dealership has what they want and need and you are confident that you are the one who can help them with their choice.

Ask them to describe the car, the exact car that they want. You have to remember this as a professional salesperson. You have got to know your inventory, while they are telling you what they want, you are thinking about your inventory, and which car best matches the description that you are hearing from the person sitting or standing across from you. You are the professional, so you have to produce the best automobile you have to match what they have said that they want. If you are a professional, you have to know your business. Remember, the only reason they came to you is because they want your help in making the purchasing decision for a new automobile or used one.

˜ ™

Closing Apartment Home Leases

A**partment home leasing closing revisited.** The people coming to lease your apartment homes are associating you with the potential service and accommodations, which they are to receive while living at your apartment home community. People evaluate you, "size you up," as soon as they see you and you began to speak to them. Remember, first impressions are lasting ones.

Let me restate again this point of importance: you have to know your inventory. Know what is available. Then you learn your new prospective resident by what they say, what they wear, how they speak, and your <u>discerning</u> what they truly desire from the inventory that you have.

<u>Knowing your inventory is the only way that you can make the proper selection for your customer</u>. People enjoy having others make decisions for them. This builds respect and confidence.

Listen to them talk about the apartment they want. Then snap your fingers and say.

"I have it!"

<u>Selling is acting at its highest</u>. Acting is the highest form of selling. Describe their apartment home to them by painting a picture of the kitchen and the beautiful hard wood floors. Do not procrastinate. Send them out there to their new apartment home. Walk out in front of the office and point in the direction you want them to go. Before they leave you, make sure everyone, both husband and wife, hear you say:

Smile and Be Very Friendly

"Mr. and Mrs. Adams, get ready to move."

You talk about programming our computers, programming your customers and clients is an excellent sales approach.

You tell them:

"I want you to get ready to move. Mr. and Mrs. Adams, as you look at each room, mentally place your furniture as well. I will be here preparing your papers."

When you look out of your office window and see your customers coming back, don't sit in that office, go out there and meet them, smiling and shaking their hands. You are grinning and they are grinning. They are grinning because you are grinning and smiling.

Never ask them if they want it. Never ask them what do they think. Never ask if they want to look at more. You must know that you have selected the perfect apartment for them. There is nothing left to do but the paperwork. Your first comment should be: Give me the name that you want on the lease. When they give you the name, they are leasing. They are saying, "I want this apartment home."

You do not have to ask if they want to okay the agreement. They have given you that name. All you have to do is turn it around and ask them to okay it.

This is the time <u>you ask them for five referrals</u>. You ask while they are excited and happy about their new home.

☙ ❧

Week 8–My Daily Sales Affirmations

1. I will persevere when things appear difficult.
2. I will get my prospects to see the benefits in the service or product, which I am offering.
3. I will relate my sales presentation and close to the personality of the person in front of me.
4. I know my sales approaches and closes will not work if I have to turn them off and on.
5. I will have the buyer's interests at heart.
6. I realize my customers are associating me with the service and product, which I am selling.
7. I will know my inventory so I can make the proper product or service selection for my customer.
8. I understand selling is a high form of acting.
9. I will ask for and get five referrals.

(Proven Techniques from AC Brown's 48-Year Track Record)

CHAPTER 9

Getting Your Referrals

Chapter 9

Getting Your Referrals

Referrals

Now, how are we going to get more customers? You get your referrals before your prospective residents get what they want. Notice I haven't asked them for any money. I'm going to bring that up after I get my <u>five referrals</u>. You say to them --

"Mr. and Mrs. Nash, when I take your application to my manager, I want to make sure that the manager knows you have referred five more people that want an apartment home out here. And when I have a vacancy, I'm going to call these people and tell them you referred them to me and that you would like for them to move out here with you."

Give me the names and telephone numbers of five family members, friends, or coworkers that you think may be interested in moving into nice apartments like these."

Why did I go that way? They told me they liked what they saw when they told me the name that they wanted on the lease. And when I asked them for those five referrals, I asked them with the tone of voice just like I didn't want the people in the next room to hear what I was saying. Acting is a part of leasing. And this requires practice.

While selling real estate, I sold 10 to 15 homes per month, even when the interest rate was 17%. How did I do it? I practiced getting referrals from children as well as adults. I remember walking up to a 14-year-old and asking.

"Have you ever thought about owning your own home?"

She looked at me with a surprised look.

"You know I'm too young to own my own home."

She thought for a few seconds, then she said.

"I heard my mother and father talking about it the other day."

I pulled my little book out of my pocket and I got her parent's names and address. Needless to say, I made the sale. You practice until you perfect your approaches and your closes. <u>You can't just think about getting referrals</u>

when you walk on your job in the morning. This is your livelihood. Make it a part of you at all times.

When asking for referrals, put your pen in a writing position. Do not smile, look sincere. This is serious business. Why? Because for every action there is a reaction. Sit on the edge of your chair. Now you may not get but two, but that's better than none. Just keep doing it, and the more you do it this way, the more people are going to be sitting in your reception room.

You have got to look at it this way. You are here for a purpose. When you make that decision, it has to be a professional one. If you do not do it that way, it will cost you dearly.

※ ※

Remember this close.

"Mrs. Adams, tomorrow I'm going to present your application to my manager. And I want my manager to know that you have referred five prospective residents who want the same thing that you want. I'm going to be looking at my manager with good eye contact when I say this."

Then I say to them, "There is a process in getting approved. I will certainly help you all that I can."

<u>It is important to use the correct words in the correct tones to persuade people to do what you want them to do</u>. You'll be surprised at how that can run prospective residents off if you don't do it this way. Tell the prospective residents that you will tell your manager when you sit down with him that they have referred five people to you that want the same thing that they want.

To get your show on the road as a professional leasing consultant <u>all you need is one prospective resident who is ready, willing, and able and who wants to move into your apartment community or a resident who is already there</u>. You have to practice this technique and fit it into your personality before it will work professionally.

As a leasing professional, you are in control. When you're sitting in your office as a leasing consultant and prospective residents are steadily coming in your office and they are asking for you, you're in control. You are in the apartment home leasing business. If they hear that people are coming in that apartment office asking for you, you are in control. If they enter the reception room and see people sitting out there waiting for you, they know you as a professional leasing consultant are in charge.

The Six B's

Specialize in the six B's. Before we can find the success we seek, no matter what business you are in, we must specialize in the six B's.

1. **Be professional, dress appropriately.**
   a. You must look the part.

2. **Be enthusiastic.**
   a. Practice smiling as you talk, ensuring it looks and feels natural.

3. **Be busy.**
   a. Act as if you have things to do and places to go, because you do.

4. **Believe in your product.**
   a. Know the product's benefits.
   b. Be knowledgeable about your product.
   c. Know your inventory.
   d. Product knowledge must be presented as a benefit to your prospective resident.

5. **Be knowledgeable about your market.**
    a. Know you market.
    b. Know your customers.
    c. Know what they want and need.
6. **Be energetic about getting your five referrals.**
    a. Your referrals are your bread and butter for your future business successes.

Now that you know the six B's regardless of your business or job, you have to say something—<u>say something that will make them stop and listen to what you have to say</u>. Practice and utilize the professional sales approaches and closes found in this chapter by applying them daily on or off the job.

You must <u>practice your sales closings so that they become a part of your personality remembering not to forget the five referrals</u>. Practice on your spouse. Practice on your children. Practice on your boss. Relate well to all people and tailor each closing to that specific individual.

Success favors prepared individuals. <u>Prepare yourself by knowing and using good sales approaches and closes</u> and by focusing on the positive, including you. Get your referrals. Your referrals are your bread and butter for your business future.

Pointers To Live By

Pointers. Here are a few *Pointers to Live by*: These will add success to your life.

- **A)** Be real to yourself and your goals.
- **B)** Study and know your product and your market.
- **C)** Focus on the positive things in your life, and practice the repetition of those things.
- **D)** Write and re-write your sales pitch to fit your market and your product as perfectly as possible.
- **E)** Rehearse your presentation, practicing in front of a mirror, in front of a child, your husband or wife, or in front of one of your peers.
- **F)** Get your five referrals up front, before the customer gets what he or she wants.

If you are selling real estate, trucks, cabbage at a vegetable stand, selling Department of Defense products, got a bicycle shop, an automobile repair shop, or doing door-to-door sales, you must <u>understand the approach you need</u> to keep your customer standing there listening to you.

Why is it so important to know the approach of what you are selling to a potential customer? You have to <u>know what the benefit of your product or service is to the potential customer</u>. You then have to <u>know what it will take, what words you need to use to help the potential customer understand the benefits of your product or service</u>. You have to use colorful words and glamorous words.

Now you have something. Remember, when you have a potential customer in front of you, do not think of them as only a sale, but know <u>they represent a long-term relationship with you</u>, and additionally <u>they represent a plethora of potential customers</u> which is a new potential sales market or sales base.

‰ ࠷

Week 9—My Daily Sales Affirmations

1. I will get five referrals from each customer. Referrals are my livelihood. I will make getting them a part of my sales presentation.
2. I will make professional decisions.
3. I will use the correct words in the correct tones to persuade people to do what I want them to do.
4. I will dress professionally.
5. I will be enthusiastic.
6. I will stay busy.
7. I believe in my product.
8. I will be knowledgeable about my market.
9. I will be energetic about getting my five referrals.
10. I will say something that will get my prospect to stop and listen to me.
11. I will practice good sales approaches and closings until they become a part of my personality.
12. I will help my prospects understand the benefits of my products and services.
13. I understand my customers represent long-term relationships and new customers.

(Proven Techniques from AC Brown's 48-Year Track Record)

CHAPTER 10

Professional Selling at Its Best

Chapter 10

Professional Selling at Its Best

Professional Selling

General selling. Let's talk here now about selling anything and everything, general selling. Because a customer may just walk into your place of business wanting you to help them. They want to purchase something, and they can't find a clerk to inspire them to buy. This is your job as a sales professional. As the professional sales person, you walk up to them—smiling—and say, may I help you? Think, perhaps they do not know what they want to purchase. Have you ever considered that? They may want to purchase a gift for someone, but do not know what they want to get them. They may want to get a piece of medium-sized furniture for a specific room, but have not really figured out what piece. It could be clothing, perfume, mascara, shoes, an aquarium or a pool table; the list goes on and on. We are sales professionals, and we are supposed to inspire people. You, the sales person have been trained with the ability to inspire people to move in specific directions; learn how— keep reading.

- <u>First, you are going to smile.</u>
- <u>Second, you are going to complement them.</u>
- <u>Third, you are going to smile as you speak.</u>

This you will have to practice so it does not seem awkward to you or your customers. (This technique works on the telephone when the person to whom you are speaking cannot see you. It is a highly effective technique.) When you see them smiling back at you, you know that smile of yours is working. As they come into your place of business, you observe the person or persons.

Perhaps a woman or a man, or a couple; are they hand in hand? Are they walking together or apart? Are they walking hurriedly or slowly? Are their heads hung low or their chins up? Is there a teenager or a young man or young woman with the couple? Or are the persons or person, young adults?

<u>You are evaluating every element and aspect of the person</u> or persons as they enter your store or department and you are mentally preparing the words that you are going to impart to them. You are going to <u>complement them subtlety and begin to tie their mind into your mind</u>. This means, you are going to begin to get them thinking the way you are thinking.

You are going to get their minds and their words to go the way you want them to go. You have just started that process with the smile and the complement. Now, anything and everything you do and say in which your customers are interested continues the process of getting their minds to follow your mind. <u>Include any positive human common denominators in your interaction with your customers in order to continue the process</u>. This sale is now moving. You have a sale moving; moving in the direction in which you want it to go.

I can guarantee you, I promise you that your cash register will begin ringing like never before. Can you hear it? <u>In order to connect your mind with their minds—smile</u>. It is so simple; compliment them on their clothes, on their style, on their shoes, on their intelligence, their panache. Compliment them on how they are wearing whatever they are wearing (including the perfume), and smile at the same time you are saying it. Do you think you can sell this way?

When you start smiling, you start selling. Your customers are going to start smiling also. Have you noticed, as you travel from place to place, how successful people are always smiling with a pleasing personality? Have you ever seen a person that is succeeding, that is not smiling?

Have you ever wondered why every man and every woman that is successful is smiling? Have you ever wondered how it is so and why they are smiling? Have you ever noticed how friendly they are? Every man, every woman, and every person on this earth is equipped with the ability to smile or to laugh. These are health boosters for you and your clients.

You will want to use common physiological behaviors and characteristics of humankind to connect with one another in an attempt to make a sale of your product or service. These common human denominators are important for persuading people to follow your sales directives, to get them to purchase the products which you know they have come into your place of business to get.

Handshakes. Let me give you an example about handshakes; don't use a vice grip, no. Do not use it. It will turn off your customer. Use a smooth, firm handshake. <u>Let there be no air between the palm of your hand</u> and the palm of theirs. You want to <u>smile and shake their hand</u> at the same time. As you look them directly in their eyes, you have begun the example of what I'm talking about—connecting their mind with your mind.

I was the manager of my Real Estate company in Atlanta. Often, I would walk into my office and shake the hands of any salespersons there and the customers sitting in the waiting room. You can do this too regardless of what you are selling—smile and greet each and every customer as if you are running for a political office.

What you are doing is selling your company, your product, or service with that smile and with that handshake. Some of the people sitting there may not be your customers, but know this important piece of information, you are selling your company, you are selling the owner, and you are selling your product or service when you meet and greet those people sitting around your waiting room.

∞ ⋈

Professional Sales Person

I want you to picture a woman in a downtown clothing store approaching the women's clothing department. She wants to purchase a nice casual dress. She is going to a casual affair at a co-worker's home. The occasion will accommodate indoor and outdoor activities. She wants to wear something new. She does not know what color or style of dress she wants to purchase. The season is mid-spring approaching summer in southern United States and she has money in her pocket. She has a budget, but money is really no object for her.

Instead of standing around finishing a conversation when the "sale" walks through the door, leaning on the counter waiting for a suggestive "I-need-some-help" glance, or following the "sale" around the store, you stop what you are doing and make professional sales evaluations concerning the person as soon as they enter.

In some stores these days, a customer is "hard-pressed" to find a sales representative to help. A sales clerk should be readily available, but not trailing you around the store as if you are a common thief. When the economy is poor, many stores will not have enough employees to handle their customer base; or the store's policy is designed not to professionally accommodate its customer base. I am not talking about those stores here.

When the sales clerk sees the person coming into the store, he begins "sizing" him up; based on his/her first appearance. What are they wearing? How are they wearing their clothes? <u>You are evaluating their posture, their attitude, how they carry themselves, the speed of their gait, and who is with them</u>. What you are really doing is being a "match-maker." First, you compile a basic profile about them in your mind, and then you wait for them to tell you what they came into the store to purchase. When they speak, you make evaluations concerning the person, their personality, education, cultural background, and past, present, and future plans. Your good evaluation will surely lead to a close.

Sometimes when you are not busy with a customer, you and another member of your sales team can practice and fine tune each other's evaluations of customers to help one another perfect this important sales technique. At first, focus on the one product. Then you want to adjust your focus to the accessories, which accentuate that first product (or service). Think multiple selling opportunities. You are looking at colors, styles, provocative nature—does the person have an extravert personality or are they introverted? But remember, your focus is on selling the one product initially.

※ ※

An Informative Example

Another informative example.

"Mrs. Adams, I have completed the test and I discovered that you need an operation," says the professional doctor.

You could not pay this professional doctor to say to Mrs. Adams: "Now before I operate, here are two other professional doctor's business cards, they are specialists as I am. I would like you to go and let them run some tests also, then you can make a decision on which doctor you want to use."

You could not pay this doctor with that white coat on to do it that way. The professional doctor makes decisions for his patients. What about the professional sales person?

Your clients want you to make decisions for them. People hate to make decisions. You must know your product or your service so you can help your clients make the best possible decisions. <u>A good professional takes charge</u>.

The professional doctor's business is based on his professional medical knowledge and based on his patient's lack of knowledge and their desire to get served by a professional who has their interest at heart. Someone who can heal them. They are waiting for the doctor to tell them something, preferably something positive. The doctor is going to give the patient an answer though sometimes it may be the wrong answer. People are generally happy with the answer the doctor gives them, because <u>they trust the doctor's judgment</u>.

There are two things the patient wants: 1) an answer as to why he is there, and 2) a prescription for what ails them. Most of the time, they may only need to change their diet and get some exercise, drink plenty of water, and they will get better. However, the professional doctor is in the business of serving his patient's interests; and his interests as well. If no one is sick, he has no business. He has to keep them coming back. As long as the doctor tells the patient to come back, they will keep coming back for more tests or for general examinations. This makes the patients feel confident that their ailments are being healed and should they get sick, they have a professional who knows how to take care of them.

The professional doctor takes charge, and people love that. He will prescribe you medicine that can help you. Like I said before, the professional doctor has all the answers, he takes charge of your health, and you love the doctor for that. People love it when professionals who know their business and who are successful in their business, give them advice which they believe will improve their lives.

Get Smart Never Settle for One Opinion

A professional doctor once told my wife that she had high blood pressure. He wrote her a prescription, which she never filled. She went home and read some books on how to lower high blood pressure. She did not get her prescription filled. She followed her knowledge from the books, ate colored fruits and vegetables, did more walking, did not allow things to stress her out; and guess what?--her blood pressure lowered to normal.

When she asked the doctor how long she had to take the medication that he prescribed for her high blood pressure, his response was, "Maybe for the rest of your life." He also asked her to come back after taking the medication for thirty (30) days. They always make an appointment for you to come back. Think about that true story. Think about your life.

The reason those patients are there at the professional doctor's office is because he is making decisions for his patients. As professional sales people, automobile sales people, as apartment home leasing consultants, <u>we must help the customer make the decisions</u>. People hate to make decisions. They enjoy having professionals think for them. Get smart. Know your products or services well enough so you can help your clients make good decisions.

ಸು ಡಿ

I want to say something here, that's really unusual about the business of selling. <u>You have to think about selling and prospecting regardless of what you are selling or to whom you are selling</u>, because the person who is sitting in front of you or standing is observing you as a salesperson. Moreover, they hear every word that you are saying, and they see everything that you do. Now what am I saying here—practice.

Practice your approach, because when you are dealing with people, your words will come automatically when you go into your sales presentation. Your transition from your normal conversation into your sales presentation must be seamless. Your customers hear every word, and they see everything that you do. <u>Make sure that everything that you say and do is pleasing to your prospective buyer.</u>

It is so easy to lose a sale. I can go into your waste paper basket and find contracts that should have been executed, but a mistake was made by a salesperson. They did not realize that they had made a mistake, nor did they realize it was their fault. They missed it by just a few bad statements or words. That same situation could have been closed effectively. They did not obey the rules of the sales game, which are as simple as drinking a glass of water when you know and practice your sales approach.

☙ ❧

Week 10 – My Daily Sales Affirmations

1. I will smile and complement my prospects and customers; smiling as I speak.
2. I will evaluate my prospects as I approach them.
3. I will be the good professional and take charge.
4. I will work towards getting people to trust my judgment more.
5. I will help my customers make the best decisions.
6. I will think about selling and prospecting for business as often as possible.
7. I will practice my approaches and closes until they become a natural part of my conversation.
8. I will ensure that everything I do and say is pleasing to my prospective buyer.

(Proven Techniques from AC Brown's 48-Year Track Record)

CHAPTER 11

Trigger Your Customer's Imagination

Chapter 11

Trigger Your Customer's Imagination

Taking Risks
Using the Right Man

My partner, M.J. Reese, who is my brother-in-law and I bought the 85-unit Cascade Cabana Apartments Homes on Dolphin Drive in Atlanta, Georgia. After we bought those apartments, we discovered there was a serious shortage of cash flow. We only had enough cash flow to hire one person. This person had to do everything. He had to do all the maintenance, including the grounds, collect rents, and lease apartments.

I put an ad in the Atlanta-Journal Constitution for an apartment manager. I had <u>asked God to give me someone</u> who could do everything, a property manager and a maintenance man combined. When Bobby Little came into my office for an interview, he was trembling, he was shaking; he was a recovering alcoholic.

God said, "Put him on the job."

Bobby Little was filled with "can'ts."

"Mr. Brown," Bobby said, "I can't paint. I can't collect money. I can't mow the lawn. I can't do this. And I can't do that."

I thought to myself, *"How can I hire this man who is filled with "can'ts?"* I thought this to myself as another little voice within said, *"Send him home."* Following my intuition, I hired Bobby even though I felt this decision to be rather risky.

This recovering alcoholic, this shaking man was ever so nervous and had never managed apartments before. Before we hired Bobby Little, our vacancy rate was 40%. A client came by wanting to buy these apartments. He gave me a very low offer. I knew I had to do something. I had to fill the vacancies in order to get a good offer. <u>Whatever you are selling, get it ready first</u>. Make it attractive to your perspective buyers.

Bobby was eager to learn everything that he could about

his new job. He put himself into it completely. I met with him every morning. He learned the approaches and closes necessary for leasing. He would watch electricians, plumbers, and HVAC technicians in order to learn their skills. With the help of his tenants, he kept the grounds spotless. He took special interest in getting a vacant apartment home ready for his new move-in. Cleanliness and those beautiful hardwood floors were in top order. Anyone of you reading this book would readily live in one of his apartment homes.

The lesson to learned here is, once you start your business, be sure to <u>hire help that will do the job better than you would do it yourself.</u>

I placed an advertisement in the newspaper which read: *"Two and three bedroom apartments for rent. Move in ready. Beautiful hardwood floors. Only 650 per month. Come and see for yourself. Please, blow your horn four times."* The advertisement read *"blow your horn four times"* because Bobby was not sitting behind a desk. He was always working in an apartment. Remember, he did maintenance and everything else.

Bobby Little accepted what I was teaching him and fitted it into his personality; he could talk about those beautiful hardwood floors so convincingly. Just think, a recovering alcoholic, why could he do it? He knew how to listen and put what he learned into practice. You can also.

The advertisement plus Bobby's convincing tone of voice triggered the prospect's imagination. Therefore, they came. They would blow their horns four times. Bobby would stop his maintenance work and lease the apartment home. In six months, all vacancies were completely filled and we had a waiting list.

> Our Job is to Solve Problems.
> The Key is Faith

Two German men from Canada, Mr. Winkles and his son came out to look at the apartments to purchase them. They were so excited about the condition of the community, as well as Bobby, that they bought this apartment home community without hesitation at a very good price. When they came, Bobby had developed into a real professional. They watched him in action and would not close unless the package included Bobby Little as well.

What was so exciting about this man Bobby Little was, he was a one-man show, managing eighty-five apartment homes. Guess what? Bobby Little went with the package. The lesson we learned from this experience is: Do not give away nor sell what you own too quickly. <u>The keys to</u>

success is faith, patience, and hard work. Get your product ready, trigger your prospect's imagination.

Our job is to solve problems. We have a tendency to run from problems--our own problems and the problems of other people. Our job is to solve problems. That is the way you make your fortune. Take a problem and turn it into millions.

‮ ‬ ☙   ❧

Apartments According to Income

Let me say it for what it is worth. We have to be doing what Jesus Christ did when He walked this earth. Not just reading our Bibles, hearing the Word preached, tithing our money and giving offerings--no, we do have to go further than that. We must use our creativity and imagination. We must ask ourselves, *"What do I want to accomplish here?"*

Let me give you an example. I owned Glenwood Village Apartments, one hundred and fifty units. I had trouble filling the vacancies during the first year. I got an idea.

Rent according to income.

I placed an ad in the newspaper. This is the way I worded my ad. *"We rent these apartments according to INCOME"*. And that stood out in my ad in caps: "WE RENT THESE APARTMENTS ACCORDING TO INCOME".

This is quite true because if a prospect cannot afford a two-bedroom apartment, he may be able to afford a one-bedroom apartment.

When you bring a prospective resident in, the first or the second question you ask is: *"What is your income?"* The prospective resident cannot deny that you are going to ask that question. He expects you to ask that question.

When I ran this advertisement, my incoming calls tripled. It is true; the prospects that called were thinking they were going to get a deal. We have to understand it this way – <u>we have to try things.</u> Many times, it is what we say and how we say it that makes the difference. <u>Use your imagination to create an inviting circumstance for both you and your prospect.</u> The prospective residents benefited by moving into highly-serviced quality apartments which they would not have seen otherwise. I benefited from their residency.

If you are not getting the desired results, try a new approach, or go down the tubes. It is often said that insanity is doing things the same way and expecting different results. <u>Do things differently to get different results</u>; the results that you need and want.

Now, write a convincing sales presentation to fit your product or service. You have got to have the words and you have got to have them right. You can't just sit there and ad lib and say anything—oh, no. You will be surprised at what you can do with a good sales presentation. You should have a telephone sales presentation and a sales presentation for one-on-one prospects standing in front of you. <u>Practice, practice, practice</u>.

I always prepare a sales presentation, no matter what I am selling. I ask the Lord to give me the right words. Then I practice the presentation until I get it just right, practicing on employees, family members, or friends. Take your sales presentation and adapt it to your situation. Use it and revolutionize your apartment home leasing business or whatever kind of business you have.

"WE RENT ACCORDING TO INCOME," this is an example of how five simple words aroused my prospect's imagination.

Earn As You Learn

As a Real Estate broker, my job was to recruit new salespeople. As we all know, new recruits are the lifeblood of an organization. We held a seminar each month, with very few attendees. As a result, recruiting was an uphill struggle. One morning I heard these words: "Earn as you learn." I put out flyers and ran an ad in the newspaper. From then on, I had a full house at each one of my seminars.

People were begging me to go full-time. They would call every two or three minutes making reservations to attend a seminar. Not only did they attend the seminars, many of them passed the Real Estate exam as well. Just those few words made all the difference: "Earn as you Learn." We are talking about triggering the prospect's imagination.

Having many full-time real estate agents, I was able to screen carefully. As a result, I set up a thriving successful business. When you read my books, you are going to learn how not to dwell on the negatives such as: bad credit, sickness, and disease. When you start thinking the way I teach you, your life will not be the same.

Rent To Buy

We are talking about triggering the prospective customers' imagination and getting them to perform in a positive beneficial way for them. Here is an example. As an investor, if you own the property you can use "RENT TO BUY", but you have to know how to use it. You have to be willing to go either way the prospect wants to go. This means they are coming to "Rent or to Buy."

Example: you prepare two packages, one for "rent" and one to "buy." You have to do your homework. When they come to discuss the transaction, you present them with facts--renting versus buying; monthly payments, taxes, depreciation, and the overall benefits.

As a professional, present them to your clients and compare what the rental versus the mortgage payments on the home will be and when they compare the two, under your direction, with the documentation, they may be able

---
When We Talk Their Benefits We Sell People What They Want
---

and want to buy even though they never thought that they could. You are performing a tremendous service here by helping people invest in home ownership.

As a professional, it is usually better to encourage buying if the client is willing, able, and ready. You will discover that if you <u>have the correct words</u> and you <u>use them correctly</u>, you can take the buyer the way that benefits them most. But you have got to be talking their benefits. It is just as simple as that. If they qualify to buy, then make your presentation so attractive, that they will want to buy. The more you practice your presentation, the more buyers will invest in home ownership.

You have to know how to sell if you use this technique. The words have to be right and you cannot ad lib. Put your script together and practice it but keep in mind that the prospect is listening attentively to every word. <u>If you have the right words and speak them convincingly, you will be amazed at what you can do</u>. Rent to buy requires practice, drill, and rehearsal.

☙ ❧

Week 11—My Daily Sales Affirmations

1. I will ask Father God to assist me when I run into roadblocks.
2. I will make my products as attractive as possible for my prospective customers.
3. I will pursue success by applying faith, patience, and hard work.
4. I will trigger my prospect's imagination to purchase by using specific correct words in the correct tones.
5. I will prepare myself to look for and seize good selling opportunities.
6. If what I am presently doing is not working, I will try something different in order to get better results.
7. I will prepare a sales presentation and tweak it to suit my prospects.
8. I will practice my sales presentation until I know that it will lead to closing the sale.
9. I will prepare myself for success by practicing all of the suggestions written in this chapter.

(Proven Techniques from AC Brown's 48-Year Track Record)

CHAPTER 12

Wisdom In Business

ॐ ☙

Chapter 12

Wisdom In Business

A Lot of Wisdom

Over the years, I have discovered many ways of preventing loss in my businesses. My brother-in-law and sisters-in-law have taught me so much over the years. Relatives do have a lot of wisdom. One idea my brother-in-law, Marshall Reese taught me was when someone asked for a favor or a loan from my Real Estate company, ask them to put it in writing and sign a commitment. Marshall Reese had experienced a real estate salesperson asking for a loan against a commission on a house, which he thought would close soon. Marshall asked the salesperson to write the request and a commitment to repay by a certain date.

The salesperson never did return for the loan because he did not have any sale in progress. Marshall probably saved his company thousands of dollars with this one technique.

☙ ❧

I was once told by the Water Department that the water supplying my apartment community was about to be cut off because our payment was past due. I had not made the payment because the bill was much higher than I thought it should have been. They had installed a new meter, but that did not lower the bill. They insisted that I owed $40,000 for the water. I had begun the process to refinance the Glenwood Village Apartments and the Water Department placed a lien against the property. I had to do something wise and do it fast.

A lesson I learned over the years is that people are more willing to negotiate money with women than with men. Using my experience, I sent my wife Gladys to the Water Department with $10,000 cash with instructions to try and settle the account. Sure enough, Gladys was able to walk out with the account settled for $10,000. I think they just felt sorry for her. (Smile)

Choosing a CPA

I have also found over the years that finding the right CPA is a very important business decision. I <u>interview CPA's</u> before I hire one. During the interview, I look the applicant in the eyes with a penetrating look and say.

"I am going to make a lot of money, and I am not planning on paying any taxes."

Now, I know I will have to pay some taxes, but the reaction of the accountant lets me know who I am dealing with. <u>I want to make sure my accountant is going to work hard for me</u>, not just charge me for keeping my records. I also want to make sure the accountant is going to work for me, not the government.

I once had the pleasure of experiencing an Internal Revenue Service audit. The audit revealed that I owed $75,000 to the government in taxes. I never believed I owed that much money, but my CPA told me I had to pay it. I fired that CPA and got an extension by the IRS. The same thing happened with my next accountant.

Later, I hired an accountant who knew his business, and he was able to get the amount owed down to three thousand dollars after meeting with auditors and answering their questions satisfactorily. He then gave me an invoice for his fee and I told him I would pay him as soon as he got the amount owed to the IRS down to $0. However, I did not insist that he do this. I was happy to pay his fee. You must shop around for good help regardless of what your needs are. At the same time, you must be able to recognize unsatisfactory help. In other words, you must know the results that you want.

Dealing with Banks

I've learned over the years that there is a secret to dealing with banks in order to get a loan. First, you must realize that the banker is not doing you a favor when he decides to lend you money. <u>You are doing him a favor when you borrow money from him.</u>

Start a relationship with the bank that you wish to borrow money from at least one year before you need the money. Begin by opening a checking or savings account with the bank manager. <u>Get to know the bank manager</u>

very well and each time you make a deposit, take time to shake the manager's hand and let him know you are there.

Keep a good balance in your accounts and make sure no checks are returned for insufficient funds. After you have maintained a good balance for the first year ask for a small loan even if you don't need it. You have to start building the bank's confidence in your ability to pay them back. If the banker asks you to pledge your savings account against the loan, do not do it. Politely tell the banker you will withdraw your money, and deposit it in a bank that trusts you. Remind them that you have trusted them with your money, they should trust you with theirs.

You only want signature loans from the bank. You do not want to put up your assets as collateral. If there are any problems later, the bank will have your assets tied up and you will have a difficult time applying your business acumen to your current projects, because your assets will be negatively leveraged.

Now the minute your get your loan, take the money and deposit it into your savings account and make the required payments on time. After you have re-paid this loan, go to the banker and ask for a larger amount, $1,000. Again, do not spend the money. Deposit it into your savings account and pay it back as agreed. This will <u>build your banking relationship</u>.

You are now paving your new economic way. You are building trust in your banking partner. The economy may be tight, but you must make all payment in a timely manner. From time to time, check with the bank and make sure your account is reported as being paid on time.

If you have lines of credit, have been paying regularly on time, have no past due payments, and are currently paying on time; even though you may have a few old collection accounts, the lender will probably give you a loan. You kill your destiny when you are late with your payments. It shows the bank and the creditors that you are a responsible client when you pay as agreed.

૭૦ ૦૪

Choosing an Attorney

Choosing an attorney is another area in which we should apply a lot of wisdom. <u>Make sure the attorney you choose is going to work for you and will take the appropriate action on your behalf</u>. Ask him or her to <u>put in writing</u> what their plan of action is for your case before you give them a retainer fee.

Attorneys really have a tendency to talk some "good law" or "legal ease" when they are trying to get a retainer fee. And when the trial starts, you would not think this attorney was the same one to whom you paid the retainer because they seem to have lost that "legal ease," that "good law" talk. Also ask for names and telephone numbers of other people they have represented in similar cases. Call these references in order to get a good perspective of the attorney.

Once while I was looking for an attorney to handle one of my cases, I went to an attorney who said he required a $3,000 retainer. He said my case was very difficult and that he would have to do a lot of work. I went to another attorney and he handled the case without a retainer and was able to settle out of court for $200, only charging me a $250 fee. As I suggested before, you must shop around for good help. Sometimes you have to interview several professionals before you find the right one.

ഌ ഌ

If an attorney calls you to discuss a complaint, refuse to talk to him. Ask him to write you a letter stating the nature of his complaint. The way you answer that letter can help you avoid a law suit. Listen to this sound advice:

1) Do not write the letter yourself,
2) Get your attorney to answer the letter while you supervise the tone of the letter.
3) When he answers the letter, you and your attorney should look for ways you can go after the attorney's client who is threatening to sue you.

In other words, connect his client to the alleged complaint and let the letter be hard hitting. Let him know that his client has much to lose. Please understand, do not write the other attorney a "sugar-coated" letter under any circumstances. You may have to pay a retainer fee if a lawsuit is filed. If you write a sweet letter, you will be sued.

If your attorney does not agree with this approach, you should interview another attorney. <u>Learn from your experiences</u> as I have learned. Figure out ways to prevent losses in your business and trust God to help you to succeed.

༺ ༻

A Comedy Show

During the first appointment with your banker, CPA, attorney, buyer, seller, visitations at hospitals, doctor, etc., always <u>insert humor and make the other person laugh</u>. You will be surprised at what will happen. If you had a problem when you went in, laughter will certainly help to solve it. You want to practice this. <u>Practice and practice</u>. Let me give you two examples. A client of mine sued me. I needed an attorney. When I went to the first attorney, I was nervous and upset. I just talked about the lawsuit and the client who sued me. The attorney hit me head-on.

"Mr. Brown," he said, "this is going to be a bad case. I am going to need a retainer fee of $3,000 for me to handle this case. This is a bad one."

I knew exactly what had taken place. I was not calm nor at ease and I did not insert humor into my introductory remarks. I did not get him laughing. I picked up my file and carried it to another attorney one-half block away. However, this time before I went into this attorney's office I made the decision I was going to use a humorous approach.

> Laughter is Something God has Given to Everyone

I got him laughing. We both laughed together. Then he looked down at the file still laughing.

"Awe, Brown," he said, "there's nothing to this. Bring me $200 to court tomorrow. I will settle this one out of court and the attorney's fee will be $250."

ಸಿ ಅ

<u>You need to practice this</u>. My wife and I went to Emory Hospital just to take a physical. Just a simple physical. While I was parking the car, my wife went in and filled out my information sheet. Boy did she give them background medical information. How my mother died, what illnesses she had before she died; and illnesses my father had before he died, and how he died, plus information about my dead siblings. When I went in, four doctors gathered around me

declaring that I was in deep trouble; had heart conditions and accompanying ailments.

The only way I could get them off my back was to suggest that they put me on a treadmill. Let me tell you, I was on that treadmill five times. Every time I got on the treadmill, they asked me how I was doing. I would tell them to speed it up. I did it five times.

They took me off the treadmill and carried me back in the office. Now, I have never known my daddy to run around at night but I put this on him. I said to them.

"If my daddy was senseless enough to run around at night," I said to these four doctors, "he should have died with heart trouble."

Never Accept a Negative Diagnosis

They just looked at each other and laughed unceasingly. I don't even believe they sent me a bill. If you had been passing the door you would have thought there was a comedy show going on in that room. The experiences of my 48 years say, *"If you accept the diagnosis, it is all over."* I even said to those four doctors.

"If God had nerve enough to bring me here, I believe the

God I serve has enough nerve to tell me when it is time to go."

Awe, you need to practice this. Practice humorous statements before you head to that next appointment. Getting people laughing before you present your problems will take you to the stars. I want you to think for a moment. <u>Didn't God give every man and lady on this earth the ability to laugh</u>? Laughter is a common human denominator.

<u>We have everything in the world to work with</u>, but we just won't use it. We prefer going in there with frowns on our faces. If we approach life this way, we are always going to accept what man says and come out a loser.

I'm talking about how to keep the thieves out of your business. If you will take what I have shared with you in this chapter and put it into practice, the only people who will be able to compete with you are the people that have this knowledge and use it. This is serious business. Don't play with this wisdom, use it.

☙ ❧

Week 12 – My Daily Sales Affirmations

1. I will get an accountant who is going to work on my behalf.
2. I will remember I am doing the bank a favor by borrowing money from them.
3. I will focus on building a positive relationship with my bank.
4. I will use an attorney who is going to make appropriate decisions concerning my case.
5. I will learn from both my positive and negative experiences.
6. I will insert humor in my approaches and conversation.
7. I will practice my sales approaches and closes; practicing them again and again.
8. I will never accept a negative diagnosis.
9. I will use laughter to help people become more positive and help maintain that positive demeanor.
10. I will take what God has given me and use it to become successful in life.

(Proven Techniques from AC Brown's 48-Year Track Record)

EPILOGUE

Eleanor Thought She Had Security

Eleanor had a good job with a good salary and full benefits. One day I asked Eleanor, why don't you learn the business of selling? I wasn't criticizing her for her type of employment, but encouraging her to learn the business of selling. Why? Because I have been dealing with the business world for 48 years and I have never heard of a good salesperson getting laid off. Eleanor replied, "AC, I am doing all right. I have a good job at the data processing company. I get sick leave, vacation pay and I'm working on my retirement fund. Furthermore, my supervisor can't get along without me."

A few weeks later, my wife and I spent the weekend at her home. That Monday morning we watched Eleanor send her kids off to school. I noticed that she was not rushing off to work. Thinking she had the day off, I asked her, Eleanor, how many vacation days are you getting this year? As she stood over the stove with her back to me, there was complete silence.

Finally, as she turned around, I noticed her eyes were filled with tears. She said, "AC I've been laid off. I don't know what I'm going to do. I got my last check on Friday. I haven't even told the children yet. This is Frankie's last year in high school and he has big plans for college next year. My mortgage payment is due the first of the month and the car payment is due on the 10th. How could they do this to me?" By this time, tears were really flowing. She ended with, "I've been on that job for twelve years".

Suddenly, I was not hungry anymore. I got up from the table and put my arms around her as I tried to find words to console her. I was so choked up that I couldn't say very much. While driving back home, I wondered about "the sick leave, the vacation with pay, and the supervisor who couldn't do without her".

What about her mortgage payment and car payment? What about Frankie's college plans? I thought if Eleanor had only taken time out to learn the business of selling while she had that job. When the supervisor brought her that last check, she could have said to him, "I have nothing to fear because I prepared myself with the business of selling."

What if Eleanor had just taken time, while she had that good job, to learn how to sell, that day when the supervisor gave her that last check, she would have said to herself, "I have nothing to fear, because I have prepared myself and everyone in my household has prepared themselves and we can make more money than we have ever made before selling anything and everything. And every one of us know how to acknowledge God and let God direct our path so we can accomplish everything we want to accomplish in life doing it God's way.

※

DO NOT LET THIS HAPPEN TO YOU!

※

TAKE WHAT GOD GAVE YOU
FROM BIRTH

TAKE WHAT YOU OPEN YOUR
MOUTH AND ASK GOD FOR

HOOK THE TWO TOGETHER

GET PERSONAL SUCCESS

Made in the USA
Charleston, SC
06 February 2011